260 mc

40 + 75

84

This book on Fiji provides a fascinating case study of planning in which the small scale and isolation of the economy enables major issues to be seen in almost laboratory-like clarity. In particular it throws light on problems of a multi-racial society in which some important economic and political roles are racially differentiated, and it illustrates the special difficulties of modernisation and growth where a major component in an economy is affluent by reason of a subsistent agriculture that does not earn a monetary income.

For the student of Fiji, it provides an authoritative introduction to a political economy on which little else of a comprehensive nature has been written in recent years. For the tens of thousands of visitors to Fiji every year it provides an opportunity for deepened appreciation and understanding of a country that has aroused their interest. For the people of Fiji, and for those in many lands who follow with interest and concern the affairs of this beautiful and fortunate country, it provides a careful and easily understood analysis of problems the understanding and ultimate solution of which are of vital and immediate practical urgency.

Price in Australia $1.95

The Political Economy
of Independent Fiji

The Political Economy of Independent Fiji

E. K. Fisk

RXTSA

Australian National University Press
Canberra 1970

Printed and manufactured in
Australia
Registered at the General Post
Office, Sydney, for transmission by
post as a book
Library of Congress Catalog Card no.
National Library of Australia Card
no. and ISBN 0 7081 0217 4

To my wife

Foreword

IN THIS YEAR of Fiji's independence, it is a particular pleasure to write a foreword to this book—the latest (but not, I trust, the last) of a long series of contributions by members of the Australian National University to the understanding of a country beautiful, friendly, lovable, but ridden with most complex problems. Perhaps I may be pardoned if I begin by reviewing the series, in a very roughly chronological order.

Early in the history of the University were W. E. H. Stanner's Fijian chapters in *The South Seas in Transition* (1953) and Carleen O'Loughlin's pioneering work on national income, followed by Adrian Mayer's studies of the Indian community and the first really professional census by Norma McArthur in 1956. Towards the end of the decade came the work of Francis West on the Fijian Administration, of Roger Frazer on land-use in Ra (one of the few studies straddling the Fijian/Indian dichotomy), and my own on the economic problems of the Fijian people. In the 1960s there were K. L. Gillion's book on *Fiji's Indian Migrants* and Alastair Couper's thesis and official report on ports and shipping, topics so important to an oceanic island group. Deryck Scarr studied the history of the Western Pacific High Commission, J. S. Whitelaw the urban geography of Suva, and I. S. Chauhan the sociology of Labasa. Peter France came to us from Fiji to write his very perceptive history of a central theme in Fijian life, *The Charter of the Land.* Very recently Russell Mathews has given authoritative advice on the taxation structure, and I have again been associated with an official inquiry, that by the Fiji Education Commission of 1969, as well as with the early days of the University of the South Pacific.

Apart from this record of work by one-time students or currently serving staff of the University, we can take pride in that of those once associated with us or soon to join our ranks: Cyril Belshaw, Gerard Ward. We have also had the pleasure of welcoming Fijian scholars in the persons of Joe Kamikamaca and Isireli Lasaqa.

The links between Canberra and Fiji are thus close and cordial. Some of us have begun or built up our reputations on Fijian work, and it goes without saying that this would not have been possible without the hearty co-operation of the people of Fiji—Fijians *sensu strictu*, Indo-Fijian, and 'Other'—and of its Government, which indeed in some cases has invited or even subsidised our inquiries, even though the results were at times critical (but in a constructive spirit) of governmental activity. To both people and Government, therefore, our warmest thanks are gladly accorded; and we in ANU—and more particularly in the Research School of Pacific Studies—take much pride in this perhaps unique association. Long may it prosper!

The Political Economy of Independent Fiji will certainly hold a distinguished place in this series, by virtue of its clarity, realism, and humane feeling. Very few books on the problems of economic development can be found that are written in such a pellucidly simple style, with an entire absence of jargon and of rhetoric, but not at all without sharp and pointed phrase and illustration— witness, amongst other instances, the extended metaphor in Chapter 6 of the Fijian ship of state on its reef-strewn seas. Indeed, the temptation is to quote and quote again. But this simplicity is not the simplicity which avoids issues or tries to slide over gnarled and intractable problems in a few easy epigrams.

On the contrary, the book is a realist critique of a vast over-simplification which lies at the base of a good deal of 'developmental' writing: the mystical belief that if only GNP or income *per caput* or capital inflow or some other monetary index carries on rising at a satisfactory rate, then all is well and all things shall be added. The present discontents of the more developed countries of the world might well give us pause before we blithely accept the unstated premiss of 'development'—that all mankind shall do the same things in the same way. The opening of Chapter 6 is a devastating comment on this easy view of life; a reminder that when economics set out on an independent course—much in the manner of Fisk's ship in which all the emphasis is on perfecting the engine and little on the navigation—it lost much, the much implied in the old term 'Political Economy', so properly used in the title of this book.

It is much easier as a matter of administration to apply the techniques for straightforward development on the indices mentioned above than it is to hammer out the very difficult new techniques adumbrated in Fisk's last chapter. It is also much easier as a matter of politics—in the short run. It is relatively easy to supply, and to point with pride to, main roads and tourist hotels and even import replacement factories. 'But a bold peasantry, their country's pride'—to supply that is indeed a Herculean labour, but in the long term it is that or nothing (nothing but disaster, that is) for Fiji and for many another small country similarly situated. The difficulty arises from many factors. One is administrative, the fact that capital must be deployed in small packets: there are many points of attack on fluid fronts. (This is not at all inconsistent with Fisk's advocacy of the 'big push'.) But most important of all, of course, is the difficulty of securing a revolutionary change of intangible attitudes in the minds and hearts of those conditioned by generations of traditionalism and Custom and—in the Pacific at least—by affluent subsistence farming. The societies are too small to stand out against the tides of modernisation, too set to yield easily.

It must be conceded that there is much that is discomforting in *The Political Economy of Independent Fiji*. But clear straight thinking on such matters is very rarely comfortable. The one certainty is that without such thinking, and action upon it, the last state of affairs is likely to be most exceedingly uncomfortable for all concerned. To this thinking, in my opinion, Fisk makes a powerful contribution, not only by the realistic quality of his analysis but by the almost classic elegance with which it is presented, and the humanity of the feeling which underlies it.

No doubt the size of the cake is basic to the problem; but, as Fisk insists, also basic is the way it is sliced. If top, middle, and bottom layers are not shared by each group, trouble is in store. Put at the mildest, and in economic terms only, if sugar is virtually Indian-only, bush crops virtually Fijian-only, big commerce virtually European-only, the temptation to think one's own sector is the only really serious one will be strong. Carried over into politics, this could be disastrous socially as well as economically. Not only expansion, not only diversification, but interpenetration of each sector of activity (and not only economic activity) by each of the ethnic groups is essential if Fiji is to be a healthy and happy state.

It cannot be denied that the remedies here proposed are drastic to all three parties. The Europeans must accept a radical change in their economic attitudes, which are quite as 'traditional' as those of any Fijian villager (though on a different level and scale), by accepting that the standard indices of growth and prosperity are not everything. The Indians must admit Fijians to a greater share in just those fields in which, by admirable effort, so many of them in three generations have bettered their condition from indentured coolies to substantial farmers and businessmen and public servants. And the Fijians must see that sitting tight on Fijian land Reserves may, in the not so long run, be simply sitting on the safety-valve of an overheating engine. If the remedies are severe, the disease, of which the symptoms are already incipient, could very easily be mortal. It may be that these are demands too rational for imperfect humanity to accept. If this be so, and one must pray that it is not so, it becomes very difficult to greet Fiji's independence with the joy that such an event should bring.

The analysis of Fiji's political economy in this book is astringent, not least in the way in which the consequences of the obvious fact that there are three Fijis are brought out. The recommendations draw on the fund of experience in other developing countries; experience which, it is often overlooked, includes successes as well as failures. They are constructive suggestions; to build upon them will call for an effort which will have to be moral and psychological quite as much as administrative, fiscal, and managerial. For these reasons I most warmly commend the book to all who love Fiji; and who that has ever lived and worked there can fail to love the land and its people?

O. H. K. Spate

Canberra
April 1970

Acknowledgments

A NUMBER OF INSTITUTIONS and a great number of individuals gave me assistance and many kindnesses while the material for this book was being assembled, and to them I wish to express my sincere thanks.

The University of the South Pacific, whose guest I was once in June 1968 and again, for some months, in 1969 provided a base from which to work and a delightful house on the campus for my family and myself. The Vice-Chancellor, Dr Colin Aikman, and his staff, including particularly Professor L.V. Castle, Professor. R.C. Honeybone, and the Registrar, Mr S.F. Perrott, gave assistance in many ways. My friend and erstwhile colleague, Professor R.G. Crocombe, has greatly influenced my thinking (often against my will) in many discussions and arguments in which I benefited from his deep knowledge of the Pacific peoples.

The Fiji administration has been at all times most helpful and forthcoming. Special mention must be made of Mr G.L. Mortimer and Mr J.N. Kamikameca, without whose sustained help and wise counsel I could have achieved little. I have also benefited from long and fruitful discussions with Mr R.T. Sanders, Mr R.M. Major, Mr B.V. Davis, Mr R.C.G. Strick, Mr A.G. Brown, Mr J.R. Bruce Lockhart, Mr G.S. Mataika, and with the manager of the Fiji Development Bank, Mr J.D. Ward. Many kindnesses were received from Mr H.P. Ritchie, Mr R.V. Cole, Mr W.W.A. Miller, Mr E.H. Jones, and Mr G. Watkins and from many other government officers.

The Emperor Gold Mining Company gave me generously of their time and facilities and I wish to thank Mr A. Watson, Mr O.H. Marshall, and Mr E.B. Turner for their hospitality and many kindnesses. I am particularly grateful to Mr R.H. Yarrow J.P. who gave me generously of his valuable time, and from whose unequalled knowledge of the mining labour force I gained great benefit. I also owe a great deal to the committee members of the

Fiji Mineworkers' Union who put up with my questioning with such patience and good grace.

I also received unreserved assistance from Mr J.C. Potts and Mr G.R.M. Day of South Pacific Sugar Mills, despite the pressure of their preoccupation with the Denning inquiry, and from Mr S. Snowsill, field superintendent of the Cane Development Scheme at Cuvu, who gave me the benefit of his intimate knowledge and deep understanding of the problems of many small-scale cane producers. Another to whom I owe a substantial debt is Mr T. Collins, of the Mbarave Co-operative, Nadroga.

In the field of commerce and industry many executives and businessmen gave me the benefit of their experience, and special mention must be made of Mr J. M. Headstrom and Mr D. Crowe of Suva, and of Mr Clark of Korolevu, who were particularly helpful. In the rural areas the numbers of Fijian and Indian families from whom I received hospitality and courteous consideration were very large and only a sample can be recorded here. They included Navitalai Ragina, Mateo Baraiooai, Beniamina Mate, Inia Seniloli, Isekeli Roko Waga, Dulip Singh, R. Nair, Aloisius Moko, Vincent Tovata, Mosese Gasewa, Ratu Baka Tavuto, R. Shankar, K. Ram, M. Khan, and many others.

In the actual preparation of the manuscript invaluable help was rendered by my Research Assistant, Mrs Maree Tait.

Finally, I am indebted to Professor Sir John Crawford, whose continuing encouragement and support made this project possible, and to Professor O.H.K. Spate, from whose masterly *The Fijian People: Economic Problems and Prospects* I, like so many others, gained my first real insight into the human and economic problems with which that lovely country is beset.

Contents

1 Introduction

WHEN ANY COUNTRY attains independence, after nearly a century of colonial-type government, a keen look at the economy in its social and political context is certainly warranted. For Fiji, such an investigation is particularly necessary, and of unusual interest.

From the point of view of the orthodox economist, the features of the Fiji situation that would first attract attention are the islands' unusual degree of isolation from the main markets and population centres of the world, the relatively small size of Fiji as an economic unit and the growing pressure of population on the limited areas of arable land, and the dominant position of the sugar industry. Particular attention would be given to increasing the exports of goods and services, to import replacement, to increasing productive capital, and to recombining the available factors of production so as to maximise the national product and increase the average level of income available for distribution.

This type of exercise is very necessary, but it is a completely inadequate basis for the formation of economic policy in Fiji. It is an approach that oversimplifies the situation by treating the economy as a single whole unit and the economic problem as being mainly that of increasing the national income. In fact the situation is very much more complex, there being three remarkably distinct components to the economy of Fiji, and as the demarcation between these economic components coincides in some important aspects with racial and political lines of demarcation, the distribution of income between these components is of great political and social importance. Moreover, Fiji is not a poor country by world standards, and consideration of all the facts (and not just the 'economic' ones in isolation) makes it clear that the most vital and urgent problem facing Fiji at the time of its independence is not so much the size of its national income, but rather its distribution.

The main body of economic thought about the problems of underdeveloped countries has been greatly influenced, naturally enough, by experience in countries like India and Pakistan, where subsistence production is in fact virtually synonymous with grinding poverty, and where the average small farmer, using his meagre resources to the full, is barely able to scrape a living for himself and his family. There the prime problems are poverty and how to break the vicious circle of lack of productivity, due to lack of capital, due to lack of a surplus for saving after minimum consumption needs are met. But in Fiji, and indeed in most countries of the Pacific region, those conditions do not prevail. In most of the Pacific, the subsistence farmer, producing from his own resources the goods and services needed for his family, is still able to produce as much as he can consume, of the main items he knows how to produce, with the use of only a part of the land and labour resources available to him. The result is that the subsistent, self-sufficient type of farmer in the Pacific can have a considerably higher standard of consumption than hundreds of millions of the poorer peasants of Asia, and can obtain this with relatively little regular work and with virtually no money income.

Historically the effect of subsistence affluence has been far reaching, particularly in Fiji. Virtually until World War II, the first premise of colonial administration was that colonial governments should be basically self-supporting. Consequently, the rapid development of local production and trade, from which urgently needed improvements in health, education, and economic services could be financed through taxation, was the first, and usually the only, path of development. This was done in Fiji, as in most other such territories, by attracting foreign enterprise, skill, and capital, which in turn combined with local surpluses of land and labour in the development of highly productive export industries and the commercial and other service industries required for their support.

However, the Fijian villager, with his affluent and leisurely way of life in his home environment, did not take with enthusiasm to the prospects of regular long hours of hard work on European plantations for a small money wage, so that the rapid development of the new industries, and thus of government revenues, was impeded by the inadequate supply of labour. This led eventually to the import of labour from a region where subsistence affluence was not the rule (that is from India), not because the ability or physique of the Indian people was superior to that of the Fijians, but simply because their motivation was strengthened by the abject poverty of their origins, so that what appeared unattractive and not worthwhile to the Fijians was strongly attractive to the Indians.[1]

There are thus three factors in the origins of the Fijian situation—the subsistence affluence of the Fijians, the entrepreneurship, know-how, and capital of the Europeans, and, subsequently, the wage labour of the Indians. In these three factors, and in their modern derivations, lie the roots of the problem of Fiji at independence. The affluence and leisurely quality of Fijian village life has been eroded, but it still exists and influences the attitudes and motivation of almost every Fijian— though the manner and direction of this influence has changed in some instances. The Indian immigrants and their descendants, now a majority in the country, are on average by no means poor, but other factors have replaced sheer poverty in sustaining their superior degree of motivation toward economic success. Much of the commerce and small industry of Fiji is now conducted, very efficiently, by Indian enterprise and capital, but the larger-scale enterprise, and in particular the large corporate organisations, remain in the hands of other foreigners, mainly European.

In the colonial situation, particularly before the development of a local representative legislature, the fact that the ultimate authority for the management of the country lay not in the hands of any one or two of the discrete local components of Fiji society but in the fiat of a remote, friendly, reasonably disinterested, and undoubtedly well-intentioned arbitrator, took much of the immediate sting and urgency out of the conflicts of interests between these components. In the long run, each component could vigorously press its claims and views, and however much it might disagree with the decision eventually reached, there was fairly widespread confidence that the decision was not based

---

1. Though it must be admitted that some early arrivals were disappointed when they compared actual conditions with the promises of the recruiters.

simply on the interests of one favoured section. With the access of independence, this disinterested arbitrator will be removed, and the decisions will be made by whichever interested party or group of parties holds political power at the time. For this reason, many of the problems of economic, social, and political policy take on a new degree of immediacy and importance.

The purpose of this book is to show not merely how the objectives and methods of economic policy need to be modified to meet the special circumstances of the Fiji situation but, in the light of the new understanding we have recently acquired of these types of situation, to reformulate the basic choices upon which economic policy formation for independent Fiji must now be based. From this, it is proposed to indicate, at least in outline, some of the measures that can, even at this late stage, be taken to implement such a policy.

The method will be first to present a moderately detailed picture of the Fiji economy, looked at as a whole and in an entirely orthodox manner (Chapter 2). This is necessary because there is no readily accessible standard work on the subject for the general reader. Chapter 3 looks behind the superficial unity of the macro-economic picture, to examine the detailed operations and characteristics of the three main components of Fiji economy and society. In Chapter 4 the political situation will be examined, with particular reference to disposition and prospects of political power between the three segments of the population, and their interaction with the economic problems and aspirations of the segments. Then follows a review of recent and current economic policy and its effects on the overall economic and political situation (Chapter 5). It will be suggested that the very success and effectiveness of this policy contain problems and dangers that in a short period of time may place the whole economic, social, and political wellbeing of independent Fiji in acute jeopardy. Finally, the last two chapters outline the manner in which economic policy should be reshaped, and how the very substantial resources available, internally and externally, may be applied in such a manner as to improve, rather than to exacerbate, the most acute and serious dangers facing the country in the early years of independence.

In this review it is necessary at times to be critical of economic policy decisions made in the past, and of many aspects of economic policy now being implemented. It must be emphasised, however, that at no time is this criticism intended to reflect on the general level of integrity or competence of those who originated or administered the policies. This criticism is made, and these new suggestions are offered, in the light of knowledge and understanding that has only recently become available, and which is in many respects still incomplete. It is knowledge derived from recent studies both of other societies with affluent subsistence sectors and of other plural societies in which racial, economic, and political differentiation has developed. These studies are now providing insight and answers to questions with which the earlier orthodoxy of economic development did not adequately deal. For example, issue will be taken with the view that the maximum growth of commerce and industry in the economy cannot be other than a good thing, because by increasing the size of the national income there will be at least a little more available for practically everyone. Though this view is criticised, it would be quite wrong to criticise its proponents for adhering to a view which seemed to have such clear support from the largest body of recorded experience with the problems of underdevelopment, and with the soundest theoretical analysis based thereon. This is the more so because Fiji has only very recently begun to have its own resident economists and planners, and these are either still in the early stages of their careers or have come to Fiji recently from other countries with different backgrounds.

It is therefore a fact of which no one need be ashamed, that the people who really knew and understood Fiji from the grass roots up were not experienced development economists, whilst those who were, not only did not have the opportunity to know Fiji in great detail, but had expertise and experience that was almost inevitably based on very different types of economic problems and conditions.

Finally, it must be emphasised that the views and suggestions incorporated in this book are also based largely on experience outside of Fiji itself. They are, however, based on long and detailed study of other economies in South-East Asia and the Pacific in which the special components of the Fiji situation have been met, analysed, and made the basis of some new theoretical tools. These theoretical tools have been tested in a study of the Fiji situation covering some eighteen months, and the results, some of which are here presented, must stand on the reactions of the people of Fiji, and on the cold light of history in the years to come.

2 The Economy as a Unity – the Large Picture

PUTTING ASIDE, for the time being, the division of Fijian economy and society into three major segments, this chapter will review the main structural features of the economy looked at as a unit seen from the outside world.

First it is necessary to examine the geographic and demographic characteristics, as these determine the physical environment in which the economy is set. The geographic factors are simple. Fiji is a small country, physically isolated from the main centres of world population and trade by thousands of miles of ocean. The land area of Fiji is itself quite limited, covering some 7,000 square miles, of which the great majority is steep and mountainous. It comprises two main islands, which contain 87 per cent of the total land area and 93 per cent of the population, but the remaining land is spread over some hundreds of smaller islands (only about a hundred of which are permanently inhabited) and scattered over nearly 300,000 square miles of sea.

The results are that Fiji's economic relations with the rest of the world are impeded by problems of both cost and speed in its transport and communications. The land area favourable for agriculture is strictly limited, and that part of it away from the main islands is further subject to the impediment of high internal costs of transport.

On the other hand, Fiji has some very favourable features. It has an equable tropical climate, with clear division into wet and dry regions, a climate which favours some diversification of agriculture. Its isolation has resulted in a remarkable freedom from some important diseases of man (such as malaria), and of animal, with which many other tropical countries are afflicted. These factors, and its picturesque setting, have combined with the likable social and personal characteristics of the peoples, and its location as a staging point on the main routes between America and Australasia, to make it attractive to tourists.

Some of the main demographic characteristics are shown in Table 1. The population has grown very rapidly indeed over the last half century, rising from 157,000 in 1921 to 519,000 in 1969. During this period the Indian population has replaced the Fijians as the largest racial component. The rate of growth of population was particularly high in the late 1950s and in the 1960s, though an encouraging decrease in the birth rate, ascribed to population control measures, has been observed in the last two years. This rapid growth rate in the recent past, however, means that the population is a very young one, and the current reduction in the birth rate will do nothing to reduce the numbers of young men and women already born who will begin to seek productive employment over the next fifteen years. The problems posed by the size and composition of the population, in relation to the restricted land and other resources available for exploitation, will be a recurring theme throughout this book.

Table 1 *Population of Fiji (thousand)*

Year	Fijians No.	%	Indians No.	%	Others* No.	%	Total No.	Estimated Annual Growth Rate †
1881	115	90	1	1	12	9	127	. . .
1901	94	78	17	14	9	8	120	− 0.1
1921	84	54	61	39	12	7	157	+ 1.2
1946	118	45	120	46	22	9	260	+ 2.7
1966	202	42	241	51	34	7	477	+ 3.3
1967	209	42	250	50	38	8	497	+ 3.8
1968	215	42	256	50	41	8	512	+ 3.0

* Includes other Pacific Islanders. Europeans, part-Europeans, and Chinese comprise 27,000 only in 1968.
† Estimates of Annual Growth Rates of Population are based on end-year figures.
Source: Derived from Bureau of Statistics, *Current Economic Statistics,* January 1970 (Suva, Fiji), T3, 3.

For an indication of the overall performance of the economy, and to assess the general level of economic activity, it is necessary to turn to the estimates of the gross domestic product, which are now made annually by the Fiji Bureau of Statistics. The main aggregate figures are presented in Table 2.[1]

Table 2 *Gross Domestic Product of Fiji, 1950-1968*

Year	Gross Domestic Product at current factor cost ($ million)	Annual Growth Rate of G.D.P. (%)	G.D.P. per head of population ($)	Annual Growth Rate of G.D.P. per head * ($)
1950	36.0	. . .	125	. . .
1953	50.8	12.2	160	8.6
1957	61.1	4.7	173	2.0
1962	90.2	8.1	214	4.3
1963	108.5	20.3	250	16.8
1964	115.1	6.1	256	2.4
1965	119.1	3.5	257	0.4
1966	123.4	3.6	259	0.8
1967	132.0	7.0	270	4.2
1968	140.0	6.1	277	2.6

Note: Estimates from 1963 to 1968 inclusive have been prepared on a more sophisticated basis than those of preceding years. Figures for earlier years can be taken only as rough orders of magnitude and are not properly comparable with those of later years.
* Figures for Annual Growth Rate of G.D.P. per head are based on mid-year estimates of total population.
Source: Bureau of Statistics, *Current Economic Statistics*, January 1970 (Suva, Fiji), T1, 1.

Considerable care must be taken in the use of any National Income estimates, and the Fijian estimates are no exception. It is easy to ascribe to such estimates qualities of accuracy or comparability which they do not possess, and for the Fiji estimates the process of estimation and the sources of data have steadily been refined and improved since the magnificent pioneering effort by Carleen O'Loughlin for the years 1950-3. In particular, the estimates for the year 1963 and after have had the advantage of greater resources and, as a result, more sophisticated methods, than the earlier estimates. For this reason comparison of early with later figures is unsatisfactory for some purposes. It is also necessary to keep in mind that the figures given are estimated on the basis of current prices: that is, they make no allowance for

1. All dollar figures are in Fijian currency. $1 Fijian = $A1.0288 = $U.S.1.1494.

changes in the general price level and purchasing power of money, both of which have changed considerably since the first estimates were made almost two decades ago. Finally, in Fiji, an important part of the rural product is consumed directly by the people who produce it, and is described as 'subsistence production'. This is a particularly difficult component of the national product to estimate, for not only is it invisible in the sense that it passes through no market wherein the volume of goods and services so consumed can be observed but, strictly speaking, it has no measurable money value, as there are usually no comparable market transactions to determine what the price of each item concerned would have been at the time and place they were consumed. The result is that estimates of the subsistence component in national income in different countries employ a wide variety of means of estimation, and international comparisons in particular are difficult for this reason.

These reservations notwithstanding, it will nevertheless be necessary to make use of the figures for comparisons, both over time and with other countries. Despite their limitations, the main relationships can be seen. First, it is clear that, however rough the comparability of the figures, there is a strong suggestion of economic growth in the economy throughout the period for which figures are available. Second, taking the period of best comparability of the figures—from 1963 to 1968—and correcting for price increases as indicated by the retail price index (which rose from 105.5 in 1963 to an average of just over 123 for 1968), we find that the gross domestic product rose by 29 per cent, whilst the retail price index rose by only 16.5 per cent.[2] There was certainly substantial growth here, even at constant prices.

When the even more rapid growth of population is taken into account over these years, the product per head of population at constant prices appears to have dropped very slightly in this particular period. It is notable, however, that the largest annual increase in product on record, centred on the rise in sugar prices

---

2. The application of the retail price index to the total estimate of domestic product, including the subsistence component, may in fact be an overcorrection and may understate the rate of growth at constant prices.

consequent upon the Cuban crisis, was in the year immediately preceding this period; taken over all, the figures suggest that domestic product per head, even at constant prices, has increased over the last two decades. Since the population of Fiji has very nearly doubled during this period, this is a formidable achievement.

The other fact that emerges, even from a most cautious employment of these figures, is that Fiji is not, by world standards, a poor country. On the figures available, the gross domestic product per head of population in Fiji is comparable with that of Spain in Europe, greater than that of any major African country except the Union of South Africa and Libya, and greater than that of any Asian country except Japan and Singapore. It is about three times that of India, four times that of Burma, and nearly twice that of Thailand.

Table 3 *Gross Domestic Product by Main Industries of Origin (% of G.D.P. at factor cost)*

Industry Group	1953	1957	1963	1966
Primary industry	54.1	50.9	42.8	34.8
Distribution, finance, transport, etc.	17.3	18.0	18.3	23.5
Manufacturing	9.1	10.3	12.3	12.2
Construction, electricity, and water	5.3	7.0	6.3	7.2
Public administration and education	6.7	5.7	5.4	7.6

Source: Derived from Government Statistician, *Preliminary Estimates of the Gross Domestic Product of Fiji 1950-1967* (Fiji), T2.

The composition of this product by industry of origin is shown in Table 3. Primary industry, which comprises agriculture, forestry, fishing, animal husbandry, and mining, is still the largest source of income itemised in the table, though it fell greatly in its proportionate contribution between 1953 and 1966. This fall, which has resulted from the rapid growth of the commercial and industrial component as compared with the relatively slow growth of agriculture and mining, will certainly have continued over the three years since 1966, as the tourist industry alone has more than doubled its receipts during those years. The result is, of course, that the proportion of the national income earned in the rural areas, even including sugar, has diminished very rapidly in recent years from over half in 1953 to probably about a quarter in 1969. From what was said about the growth of the national product, it is clear that although average incomes per head of population over all have probably increased somewhat in real terms since 1953, average incomes in *rural primary* industries have certainly fallen in real terms, while those of secondary and tertiary industries have certainly increased. The significance of this change in the distribution of incomes will be discussed further when the racial participation in the various industries is analysed.

International Trade and the Balance of Payments

The small size of the Fijian economy means that it must depend on imports for a wide range of the goods and services required to sustain a modern society. To pay for these, exports of some kind are necessary, whether as goods in world demand, like sugar, or in the form of services such as are rendered to tourists and to ships and aircraft staging in Fiji.

The total value of imports has risen from $35 million in 1958 to $68 million in 1968, very nearly doubling in ten years. Over the same period total exports (including re-exports) increased rather more slowly, from $29 million to $49 million, so that the trade deficit increased from $6 million in 1958 to $19 million in 1968. One of the important factors that has made this possible is the substantial earning in overseas currencies derived from the sale of services such as airport and seaport services, and the provision of transport, accommodation, and amusement for tourists. Also important is the inflow of investment capital, both private and public, which naturally tends to lead to a comparable increase in imports in the relatively short term, whilst the effect on earnings is not felt until some years later.

The composition of imports is of particular interest. Table 4 lists the imports by Standard International Trade Classification for the last five years for which figures are available. From this it will be seen that the largest items are machinery, manufactured goods, and food, with a substantial collection under the miscellaneous heading, and for chemicals and mineral fuels. Some of these categories are too broad for their figures to be very significant without further detail, but the pattern to be expected from a small, remote economy is nevertheless discernible in the heavy emphasis on categories such as machinery, chemicals, mineral fuels, and manufactured articles. The size of the mineral fuels bill is due to the amount of international air and sea traffic making refuelling stops in Fiji: in 1968, for example, there were re-exports of $4.85 million to offset against the imports of $7.3 million under this category.

Table 4 *Imports by Value and SITC Sections ($000 Fijian currency)*

	1964	1965	1966	1967	1968
Food	10,473	12,202	11,684	12,651	13,329
Beverages and tobacco	1,275	1,367	1,193	981	1,353
Crude materials	1,087	1,369	595	649	892
Mineral fuels	5,636	5,681	5,447	6,201	7,329
Oils and fats	640	861	861	759	843
Chemicals	4,152	4,574	3,830	3,927	4,993
Manufactured goods	11,185	12,280	9,865	11,093	14,074
Machinery	14,029	13,008	9,972	12,129	15,171
Misc. articles	6,131	6,091	6,137	7,281	9,174
Misc. transactions	644	729	961	621	1,244
Total	55,251	58,162	50,545	56,291	68,402

Source: Bureau of Statistics, *Current Economic Statistics,* January 1970 (Suva, Fiji), T25, 35.

Imports of food, which may seem high for a primary producing country with high transport costs, will be discussed in more detail in Chapter 3. At this stage it will suffice to note that the figure is somewhat inflated by the inclusion of $1.7 million for the import of 'fish, fresh, chilled or frozen', the majority of which represents the throughput of a Japanese factory processing fish landed by foreign-operated trawlers; this throughput then reappears again in the export figures.

Another particularly interesting feature of the import pattern, which throws light on the current pattern of economic development in the economy, is the analysis of imports at concession rates. This is provided by the Government Statistician in his Trade Report for the year 1968. These concession rates refer to imports admitted at reduced rates of duty 'in the interests of stimulating economic development', and are given in Table 5. It shows clearly that imports of capital goods and materials of categories considered by government to be of particular importance for economic development are flowing mainly into secondary and tertiary industries (and mining), on the one hand, and into the public sector on the other. Only 10 per cent is going into the agricultural sector direct. Although it is also clear that direct

Table 5 *Imports at Concession Rates ($000 c.i.f. Fijian currency)*

	Amount	%
Agriculture		
Capital goods	458	
Materials	1,394	
Total	1,852	10
Manufacturing, mining, processing and service industries		
Capital goods	5,308	
Materials	3,896	
Total	9,204	51
Other		
Government supplies (including contractors)	4,838	
Privileged bodies, etc.	2,172	
Total	7,010	39
Total All Concession Imports	18,066	100

Source: Legislative Council of Fiji, 'Trade Report for the Year 1968', *Council Paper No.11 of 1969* (Government Press, Suva, Fiji), iv.

imports of valuable plant and materials obviously play a larger part in the development of manufacturing, transport industries, mining, and the like than they do in the development of small-scale agriculture, so that there is a reason for this pattern, nevertheless the fact remains that the resources bought, borrowed, or received as gifts from abroad are flowing mainly into the direct development of the more sophisticated segments of the economy.

Exports are the goods and services that Fiji provides to people from outside Fiji, with which it earns the resources to pay for its imports. In the short term, there are other ways of paying for imports, such as borrowing, attracting foreign capital, or seeking aid from friendly countries or international agencies. For the most part, however, such devices do not wholly avoid, but rather postpone, the necessity to pay for them from exports. In the long run, a country in the position of Fiji at independence must see its way to balancing its books with the outside world, by increasing the value of the goods and services it sells to other nations, or by reducing the value of the goods and services it imports from outside, or (as is more usual) by attempting to do a bit of both.

Table 6   *Principal Exports (f.o.b.) and Tourism Receipts ($m Fijian currency)*

Year	Sugar	Coconut products	Gold	Bananas & lumber	Re-exports	Tourist receipts
1963	28.8	4.9	3.1	0.7	5.6	3.6
1965	25.0	4.9	3.1	0.4	6.9	7.4
1967	23.8	3.3	3.1	0.4	7.7	11.2
1968	24.9	5.1	3.5	0.7	9.9	17.7

Source: Bureau of Statistics, *Financial Aspects of Tourism* (21 August 1968) (mimeograph, Fiji), T8, 8.
1968 figures obtained personally from the Government Statistician.

The prospects for increasing individual exports or for replacing certain imports will be discussed in more detail later. At this point the concern is with the way in which Fiji currently earns it overseas income, through the export of goods and services in the present and in the recent past. Table 6 gives the figures for the principal exports, and for receipts from tourists, for four recent years.

From this table two things stand out particularly clearly. First is the importance of the sugar industry, which has made by far the greatest individual contribution to Fiji's overseas earnings in recent years. Second is the very rapid growth of the tourist industry as a source of overseas earnings. In the short period of five years this has risen from a relatively minor source, earning about one-seventh as much as sugar and a little over three-quarters as much as coconut products in 1963 until in 1969 it was earning not much less than sugar and four to five times as much as coconut products. Here again a significant pattern is discernible, in which the rapid growth of Fiji's overseas earnings depends firstly on the maintenance of the exports of the sugar industry (which is mainly Indian at the grower level and European or expatriate at the level of overall organisation, processing, entrepreneurship, and marketing), and secondly on the growth of the highly sophisticated tourist industry and the commercial and service industries associated with it. The industries in which the indigenous rural people are mainly involved, coconuts, gold, and bananas, are rapidly being surpassed in importance as earners of foreign exchange.

Finally, before leaving the external, international aspects of the economy, it is necessary to look briefly at the balance of payments between Fiji and the rest of the world. This exercise attempts to take into consideration not only the earnings and spendings on goods and services between Fiji and other countries, but also the less visible flows in respect of such services as insurance, profits, interest, the flows of capital, and gifts or grants between nations and between individuals. The results of this interesting, important, but rather uncertain exercise for the year 1968 are presented in Table 7. In this table, one of the key figures is the balance on current account, which appears at the foot of the table. This figure means that in the year 1968, Fiji spent more overseas than it earned or was given in grants. It was therefore running into debt. The amount involved in that particular year was about $6 million.

Indications are that this overdraft in the international account is more than balanced by movements in the capital account. Private investors have transferred substantial financial credits from overseas into Fiji, presumably because they think that the investments they have in mind in Fiji will be more profitable, after considering the risk element, than alternative investments open to them elsewhere. This seems likely to continue in the immediate future, while government and semi-government borrowing is also likely to be successful in attracting substantial amounts of additional overseas capital in the next year or two, particularly if World Bank finance for some major development programs is negotiated (as seems likely).

Table 7 *Fiji Estimated Balance of Payments with the Rest of the World —Identified Transactions—1968*

Current Account Only ($ million)

1.	Imports f.o.b.	55.4
2.	Exports and re-exports f.o.b.	39.9
	Visible balance	− 15.5
3.	Official grants (net) *	4.9
4.	Other invisible — debits	− 20.4
5.	Other invisible — credits	21.45
6.	Gold production	3.4
	Current balance	− 6.1

* Including Colonial Development and Welfare Grants and other official grants.

These resources are accounted for in money terms, but money itself, whatever the currency, is only a means of exchange and of accounting for goods and services, and the resources they represent can only be used in Fiji when, and to the extent that, goods or services are imported from overseas. Therefore, when there are overseas investors, public or private, wishing to invest their surplus resources in Fiji, the money capital flow that this causes (which appears in the accounts as a credit under capital account) can only be used as and when there is an equivalent flow of actual resources, that is of goods and services, into Fiji — which must then appear as a debit on current account. For this reason, a debit balance on current account, if balanced by a credit on capital account, is evidence of the extent to which the capital inflow is being used. In Fiji, the figures available, imperfect as they are, suggest not that Fiji has been spending too heavily overseas, but rather that it may have been spending too little to make full immediate use of the capital inflow available for its development.

3 The Economy as a Unity— Internal Aspects

CONTINUING THE ANALYSIS of the economy as a unity, but turning to the internal structure, this chapter will discuss the main components that interact in this unity, their roles in the production of the national supply of goods and services, and some of the relationships between them.

The problems and prospects of rural development will be dealt with in detail in later chapters. Here only the factors determining its place in the economy will be considered. First, the land resources of Fiji suitable for agriculture are strictly limited. It is estimated that only about 12 per cent of the land area, totalling about 500,000 acres, is arable. It might be technically possible to add to this, for example by reclaiming and bunding the mangrove swamps that fringe many coastal areas of the main islands. In such ways perhaps a further 100,000 acres could be made arable if it became economically worth the very high capital cost involved. However, there is a definite limit, and at present this stands at something under one acre of arable land per head of population. Second there is the problem of markets. The types of crop and animal products that can be produced in Fiji are also produced on a large scale in many other countries of the world. Moreover, compared with many of these countries, Fiji is more remote from the main markets, has higher transport costs, and has higher labour costs due to its generally higher standard of living and income. For many products suitable to the Fiji environment, such as sugar, coffee, cocoa, tea, there are either international agreements limiting production or there is from time to time serious over-supply in the face of inelastic world demand, with at times catastrophic falls in price. With other products, such as palm oil and rice, over-supply on the world market seems likely within the gestation period necessary to bring large-scale investment in such production to fruition.

For this reason, apart from the natural growth of that sugar market in which Fiji has, for the time being at least, a position of privilege, and apart from some occasional opportunities in which Fiji may have some special environmental or other advantage for a time over competing countries, the future of Fiji agriculture and animal production must look increasingly to its expanding home market and to import replacement, with the export (probably at lower prices) of modest surpluses. In this there remains plenty of scope, in the production of rice and possibly other grains, and to a lesser extent in vegetables, meat, dairy products, and possibly tea.

This change of orientation from the export to the home markets has only just begun, but it is of the greatest possible importance, and will require an institutional and organisational revolution as well as a technical one. Moreover, much of this revolution will have to take place in small-scale units of production, on lands owned and occupied by people who have not been at the forefront of the investment and innovation on which Fiji's past progress has been built. The capital, technical know-how, research, entrepreneurship, and services necessary cannot flow as readily into this development as they can into development in the urban areas and into secondary and tertiary industries. This applies, of course, in particular to the flow of foreign capital, enterprise, and skills, but local resources are also affected.

Components of the Internal Economy

Some of the more important components of the internal economy will now be considered.

Sugar. Although the tourist industry is rapidly growing in importance, there is no question that the prosperity of Fiji has been built almost entirely on the foundations laid by the sugar industry, and that sugar is still the mainstay of the economy as a whole. In 1968, out of total domestic exports of $40 million, sugar accounted for $25 million. Even more important, in the year of the last census, 1966, the economically active population enumerated outside village subsistence agriculture was just on 100,000 people, of whom some 30,000 were wholly or partially employed directly in the production of sugar cane or in its processing. When the indirect effects of the industry on employment are added, the dominant position of sugar in the total economy is quite clear.

The future of Fiji is therefore very much tied up with the future of this industry. To understand the nature of this involvement, and the problems and prospects of the sugar industry in Fiji, it is necessary to understand some features of the organisation of the industry.

The production of sugar cane in Fiji is almost entirely in the hands of small local farmers. In 1966 there were 15,600 separate cane-growing smallholdings of an average size of just under ten acres. The great majority of these are farmed by Indians, though by 1969 there were about 2,700 Fijians producing cane. This has come about largely as a result of a deliberate policy of the Colonial Sugar Refining Company, which set out in the 1920s to transform an estate-based cane-growing industry into one based on small independent local farmers. This policy of fostering the small grower has been continued by the subsidiary company, South Pacific Sugar Mills, formed in 1962 to take over the Fiji interests of the Colonial Sugar Refining Company.

As a part of this policy, the milling company has developed over the years a wide range of co-ordinated services that enable the small grower to produce cane of high quality with considerable efficiency. As a result the Fijian grower is able to compete effectively with other sugar industries throughout the world and at the same time to earn an income that compares favourably with most. No other sugar producing country in the world has anything like so large a proportion of its cane produced by such small independent farmers. This is only possible in Fiji because the services provided by the millers make available, as external economies to the small producer, most of the economies of scale that would otherwise be available only to very large-scale producers. These services include research, the breeding and distribution of improved varieties of cane, the development of improved cultivation practices, soil testing, fertiliser use, disease and pest control, and the dissemination of the results of this research to the individual growers. The millers employ a large number of field staff who operate what is in effect an extension service to the growers, and who help to co-ordinate harvesting and transport of the cane. They provide on credit, and distribute, fertiliser and other crop requirements, and operate various institutions that either provide credit direct to the growers or enable growers to obtain credit from other sources for repayment from their forthcoming cane harvest. They own and operate a system of light railways for the transport of the cane. Over and above this they undertake the manufacture and distribution of the product, and market it on a complex and highly competitive world market.

This symbiosis between the large foreign-owned sugar milling company and the small independent sugar farmer has benefited the company, and Fiji, for many decades. But it has also benefited the small farmer who grows the cane, for without these services and the policy behind them he would not be there. What is more, should those services cease to be available, the sugar industry of Fiji would also cease. This is of particular significance at the time of writing, for South Pacific Sugar Mills, and its Australian parent the Colonial Sugar Refining Company, have announced that under the new contract determined by Lord Denning between the millers and the growers it is no longer a commercial proposition for an expatriate company to operate this business, and that they therefore propose to withdraw at the end of the 1972 crushing season.

It is clear that this will create an opportunity for some local institution, whether government controlled, co-operative or whatever, to take over the local assets of the company on quite favourable terms. What is not clear is just what institution, and on what terms. Nor is this the place for speculation on these matters, as they will probably be well on the way to determination when this book appears. What can and must be said, however, is that not only the physical assets of the milling company, but the whole range of its expert services will have to be taken over and sustained at least at its present level of efficiency, if the industry is long to survive. This will not be easy, particularly in the relatively short time available until the milling company's decision to withdraw becomes effective. The problem will be more one of organisation and staff than of finance.[1] However, it is quite vital for Fiji to see that it is solved, and that the past highly successful complementarity between the local farmer and the Australian company is restored by a new organisation capable and willing to provide the same services and facilities with equal efficiency.

This question of organisation, therefore, is one of the major uncertainties in the future of the Fiji sugar industry. The other, of course, is the market. Fiji supplies most of its own sugar requirements, consuming about 19,000 tons a year. This is a sure market, but compared with the total production of the Fiji industry, over 393,000 tons in 1968, it is minute.

The world sugar market is, in most years, more than well supplied. The proportion of the world market supplied by Fiji is very small, about 0.5 per cent, but most of the market is very strictly controlled. Under the Commonwealth Sugar Agreement Fiji has a quota to supply the United Kingdom with 140,000 tons at a stable price which at the beginning of 1970 was substantially above the 'world' price. This position in the Commonwealth Sugar Agreement will last for at least six or seven years if the United Kingdom does not join the European Common Market, or until 1974 if it does. Fiji also has, for the time being, a small quota in the U.S. market of 37,000 tons at an even more favourable price. This small allocation, however, which was derived from the re-allocation of the U.S. Cuban quota, is due for review next year and cannot be counted upon indefinitely. Finally, under the International Sugar Agreement Fiji has a basic export tonnage of 130,000 tons, most of which goes to Canada, New Zealand, Singapore, and Japan.

There is some scope for increases in these market outlets, as increases in population and standards of living raise demand. However, such increases appear likely to be unspectacular. As a newly independent nation, Fiji may, in the next year or two, receive a somewhat more sympathetic hearing amongst the international bodies and from some large nations such as the United States and the United Kingdom, if it is organisationally in a position to take advantage of this. However, it is also quite

1. For which a loan from the World Bank, or the Asian Development Bank, should be possible.

possible that the favoured position now enjoyed by Fiji on the United Kingdom market could be lost within a few years, whilst that in the United States market could be lost even earlier than that. The outcome of all this is that there seem at the time of writing no grounds for planning for any major increase in sugar production in Fiji for the next few years, and that such increases as may prove marketable should be readily covered by increases in productivity on existing sugar land. Further substantial increases in the acreage of sugar cane do not seem to be a practicable development. On the contrary, the possibility of increased difficulty in marketing the crop, leading to less favourable prices, cannot be discounted.

The future of Fiji's sugar industry, therefore, seems to lie in sustaining and improving its efficiency and competitive position at present levels of production, rather than in expansion. In this, the effective replacement of the South Pacific Sugar Mills Company with another, at least equally efficient institution, is vital.

Timber, however, is an industry of the rural areas to which many of these reservations about sugar do not apply. It presents the prospect for productive use for very large areas of non-arable land at present unutilised and for which it is difficult to see alternative productive uses. This applies both to natural forests and to timber plantations. At present Fiji imports timber, but there appears to be a potential not only for self-sufficiency but probably also for the production of a substantial surplus, in one form or another, for export. This potential, which is still being investigated by a current United Nations Development Programme project, holds prospects of useful spread effects through the development of larger sawmills and other possible forms of processing plant, as well as through the transport requirements of the industry, especially in the more sophisticated sector of the economy.

During most of the last two decades, timber extraction and milling has been undertaken by considerable numbers of small-scale local operators, often as a part of a small diversified family business. In early 1969 there were about fifty licensed mills in operation, mostly very small, and mostly producing low-grade and unprocessed timber. The unpopularity of Fijian timber on the local market, and the consequent high timber imports, had been due to this low standard, or the complete absence, of processing—which could only be undertaken economically on a moderate or large scale. For this reason, government had commenced action to reduce greatly the number of licences and to compel proper processing. As a result the popularity of local timber has been growing as quality has improved, and the very small and inefficient producer is being eliminated from the industry. This tendency can be expected to continue with present policies and to lead eventually to the elimination of a large part of the timber imports, and possibly to the export of certain timber products. However, in achieving this improved efficiency and output the industry will become more capital intensive, will operate in larger and more sophisticated units of organisation, and will attract more foreign capital and enterprise.

Mining has a long history in Fiji, though only gold has been mined consistently on a large scale for any substantial period. There has, however, been a far-sighted policy of geological survey and provision of information to potential mining interests, and this is beginning to show results. Copper, bauxite, and off-shore oil seem to hold the most immediate prospects. There is little question that the discovery of important economic quantities of minerals could bring substantial benefits to the Fiji economy in royalties and government revenues, and to a lesser extent through the use of local service industries. On the other hand, at the present stage of development of the Fiji economy, most of the resources of capital and know-how for the exploitation of such discoveries will come from international mining corporations, and will be an 'enclave' type of addition to the most advanced and sophisticated segment of economic activity.

Manufacturing is increasing, and will continue to increase. The scope is limited either to production for the local market in products for which the economies of large scale do not give the overseas producer advantages that outweigh the disadvantages of distance and transport cost, or to the processing of raw materials both for local consumption and for export. In this there is still plenty of room for expansion, and the opportunities are not by any means confined to small-scale operations. Sugar milling provides one of the better known examples of the processing industry, though in Fiji the operations of the milling organisation go very much further than simply processing. There are others, including several international tobacco companies that buy and process leaf produced by small local farmers and now provide practically the whole of the local market supplies of cigarettes. The processing and distribution of dairy products is another field in which large international companies have growing interests, and local production of dried milk and of ghee, both large imports during the 1960s, seems likely to be an early development.

One of the problems associated with the development of local manufacturing derives from the limited size of the local market. There are many manufacturing processes for which the minimum economic scale of production is quite large, and at times there is room for only one efficient producer in the whole of Fiji. Tea manufacturing may be such a process. The present consumption of tea in Fiji is running at a little over one million pounds weight per year, mostly imported from Ceylon. This is just about the minimum amount necessary for the economic operation of *one* modern tea processing factory. Therefore, if a tea industry were to be developed in Fiji to serve the captive local market (the prospects of profitable exports of lowland tea seem unlikely to be attractive), there would be room for only one manufacturing establishment to process the whole of the crop. In this way, the development of manufacturing must, if any reasonable degree of efficiency is to be achieved, involve monopolistic and oligopolistic operations by large-scale operators. Despite the well-known dangers of such operations, it is therefore necessary to learn to live with them. This is quite possible, but it means that other deliberate institutional means have to be provided to ensure efficiency and fair pricing, and so to provide an alternative to the discipline which, in a free enterprise economy, we are more accustomed to leave to competition.

Some indication of the progress already achieved in this field of import replacement is given in Table 8, which presents figures for some industries in which Fiji is now almost self-sufficient.

Commerce and Tourism are highly developed and buoyant. The rapid growth of tourism in recent years has been a particularly strong stimulus not only to hotel and tourist services themselves but to trade and service industries in general. In addition, investment in new hotels, resorts, and other tourist facilities has had marked spread effects into the construction industry and to many other parts of the advanced sector of the economy.

Table 8 *Estimated Local Consumption of Certain Commodities, 1968*

| Com-modity | Unit | Local Product Consumption | | | | Per cent share of local pro-duction in consump-tion |
		Total local production	Local production exported	Apparent consumption of local production	Total con-sumption (including imported)	
Beef	lb	6,740,214	36,470	6,703,744	7,245,744	92.5
Pork	lb	480,619	4,865	475,754	604,443	78.7
Beer	gals.	1,057,000	8,107	1,048,893	1,174,237	87.6
Cigar-ettes	lb	1,720,120	127,168	1,592,952	1,613,891	98.7
Rice	tons	17,286	2	17,284	23,568	73.3
Cement	tons	50,000	900	49,100	49,620	99.0
Paint	gals.	200,378	25,961	174,417	213,590	81.7

Source: Bureau of Statistics.

The Public Sector is efficient and honest—particularly so for a country in this stage of development. It comprises the normal functions of administration and services, including law and order, public works, health, and education. It operates telephone and postal services, broadcasting, electricity supply, a housing commission, etc. as trading or semi-trading services. As an employer, the public service is important both for the number of its employees (see Table 11) and for the proportion in the higher income levels. As a component in the total economic activity of the nation, the Fiji national accounts for 1967 estimate operations on government current account at $25.2 million compared with private sector current account at $128.1 million, and gross public investment at $9.1 million compared with gross private investment at $20.9 million.

Banking and Finance. Ordinary commercial banking services are well developed, though there are no trading banks with headquarters in Fiji. There are four foreign trading banks established in Fiji (one Indian and three from Australia and New Zealand), and these have some two dozen branches distributed around the main commercial centres. Each of these trading banks also operates a savings bank, and the government operates a Post Office Savings Bank and a Fiji Development Bank. There is no central bank, and currency issue is controlled by a Currency Board.

This means that the main banking services are operated by institutions controlled from overseas, operating as branches rather than as autonomous Fiji banks. The Fiji government has no direct control of deposit or other ratios maintained by the banks; these and other major bank policies are determined ultimately by decisions taken overseas. Although this system has worked well and responsibly, the provision of a central banking system would add a valuable instrument for ordering the financial affairs of independent Fiji in its own interest, and would facilitate the mobilisation and allocation of resources in support of the policies of the new government. With the coming of independence, the institution of such a central banking system should not be long delayed.

The Fiji Development Bank is a valuable unit in the financial structure. It developed out of an Agricultural and Industrial Loans Board that had been operating since 1952. The services of this bank are well developed, and include a capacity for assessment of, and advice to, small business and industrial enterprises. However, the greatest advantage of this institution is the opportunity of bridging the gap between international and other major sources of investment finance on the one hand, and local productive enterprise on the other, with the security afforded by the backing of the Fiji government.

Other financial institutions of importance include the Fiji

Development Company (a subsidiary of the Commonwealth Development Corporation), and a building society backed by government and the Fiji Development Company. There is a National Provident Fund and there are funds of life assurance companies over which the Minister of Finance exercises some statutory control.

Opportunities for local investment of savings by the general public are limited. There is no stock exchange (though one is now mooted), and there has been no recent local government bond issue. Partly as a result of this, there are very few local public companies, and investment in most of the larger corporations is possible only through stock exchanges overseas. The small size of the Fiji economy, and the tradition of small family enterprise among a large part of the Indian population, are both impediments to the rapid development of such financial institutions for local public investment, but this merely affects the timing, and not the need, for their development. With the coming of independence, and with the growth in the size of the monetised component in National Income, the need for such institutions is rapidly growing.

Investment has proceeded at a high rate in Fiji for some time, and in 1967 was estimated at $29.9 million out of a gross domestic product at market prices of $143.5 million, that is at just under 21 per cent. Of this, gross public investment comprises just under one-third. Some of the important components contributing to capital formation in 1967 were:

	$ million
Undistributed company profits	4.9
Depreciation allowances	5.3
Personal saving	6.1
Government saving	2.6

Whilst this was all domestic saving, a large part of the saving under the first two items was by overseas firms. The balance of capital formation was financed through capital inflow from overseas, through overseas aid, public borrowing overseas, and new private investment.

The external public debt in 1967 was a modest $4.5 million, and there is scope for considerable further public borrowing overseas for development. Fiji has good credit standing internationally.

The Subsistence Sector still accounts for a large and important part of the economic activity of Fiji. It can be considered as being made up of two parts. First, there is a large section of the commercial farming population, mainly Indian, whose principal activities are the production of commodities for the market, but who also produce, as a sideline, most of their own food. These people are characteristically individualistic, wholly oriented towards the monetised advanced sector of the economy, and their subsistence production is usually undertaken because it pays in money terms.[2] This section does include some Fijian farmers with *galala* or 'exempted' status, who have been permitted to pay an annual commutation rate to exempt them from communal services normally required of a Fijian villager, but their numbers are relatively small.[3]

Second, there is that part of the subsistence sector that includes the great majority of the Fijian population, in which the people live in villages and farm their traditional lands in a manner that is still largely in accord with their traditional way of life. In the present-day Fijian village money is much in demand and cash crops are grown for the market, though usually on a very much smaller scale than by the independent commercial farmers. However, subsistence production is not here a minor adjunct to the cash cropping activities, but rather the reverse. Subsistence production is an important part of the traditional way of life, on to which cash-earning activities have been grafted to provide the means to village improvements that would otherwise be inaccessible or to provide luxuries not available from subsistence production. The proceeds of such cash-earning activities are seldom retained wholly by the individuals who earn them, but are commonly disposed of either communally or in large part by gift

---

2. That is, the saving in not having to buy foodstuffs is greater than the money return would be for alternative cash crops.

3. Though this status technically lapsed in 1968 with the abolition of the legal requirement for commutation, the term is still used loosely to refer to independent farmers who started out in this way.

to other members of the family, sometimes quite remote members, and to people from whom past kindnesses have been received.

Although pressure of population on land resources, leasing of land to commercial farmers, and the increasing diversion of sections of the better village lands to cash crops such as tobacco is pushing the subsistence gardens back on to land that will eventually require a substantially higher labour input to maintain the required level of production, Fijian village agriculture is still, in most areas, highly productive. With some exceptions, traditional subsistence farming provides an abundance of good traditional foods, adequate shelter, and the means for gracious traditional entertainment, at the cost of two to three days work a week. From this secure base the Fijian villager ventures into the cash economy, whether through cash cropping or through wage labour, with the knowledge that if he does not succeed or for any reason finds it convenient to stop his cash-directed activities, he can do so without great hardship. Even a senior Fijian government official, who has made his career outside his village for fifteen to twenty years, knows that he can walk out of his job tomorrow and return to his village, where neither he nor his family would ever want for the necessities of life. In this way, the primitive affluence of the traditional Fijian subsistence sector extends its influence far beyond the limits of the villages and into the heart of the advanced monetary sector, wherever Fijians may be found.

Conclusion

Looked at as a unit, the Fiji economy appears in a reasonably healthy state. Economic planning on a sophisticated scale is in the early stages, and a fairly detailed five-year plan is now more than half way through its course. The balance of payments situation is good, and a strong inflow of private capital is already in evidence. Loan finance from friendly nations, and from international agencies, is available for sound projects. Development prospects are good, particularly in connection with the booming tourist industry, and in the field of import replacement. New and quite major industries are being planned. Self-sufficiency is in sight for rice, meat, dairy products, and has already been virtually achieved in several other commodities. The national income has been rising as fast as population or faster, and population control measures appear to be taking effect. Schools, health facilities, and other social benefits are well developed, though they are, of course, concentrated most around the main centres of population and industry.

From this viewpoint, the Fiji economy is well managed and set for a period of strong, orderly growth.

Unfortunately, it is entirely misleading to look at the Fiji economy only as a whole unit.

4 The Three Fijis

THE DANGER of looking at the Fiji economy simply as a a unit whole is that it oversimplifies the situation by excluding from consideration some problems, directly affected by economic policy, that are more important and more urgent than the problem of the size of the national income. For some developing countries the extreme poverty of the national product may be such that no other problems can effectively be considered until an increase in the national income has been achieved. As has been shown, this is not so in Fiji. Under these circumstances, growth of national income deserves an important place in national policy, as a means of fostering the kind of social conditions it is desired to produce; but it is important as a means to such an end, and must not be confused with the end itself. A policy that cultivates growth of income at the cost of losing or destroying vital components of national welfare is wrong.

Of particular importance in this respect is the distribution of income between the racial groups of which the new nation of independent Fiji is composed.

In considering the social, political, and economic problems of any nation there are numerous groupings or divisions of the population that may be significant for various purposes. For example the population may be considered under divisions such as rich and poor, landed and landless, urban and rural, young and old, conservative and radical: there are many possibilities, all of which are in a sense artificial, and are oversimplifications, but nevertheless are useful tools of analysis for certain limited purposes. Similar divisions are discernible in Fiji society. There is a type of grouping in Fiji, however, that is of particular importance at this time of independence because the differences between the groups are of great political significance, vital to the division and use of political power in the new nation, and correspond with divisions and conflicts of interest in a wide range of social and economic affairs.

This grouping, which will be used in slightly simplified form here, is the division of the Fiji population into three racial groups, Fijian, Indian, and Others, which were the basis on which the 1966 constitution was drawn up. Under this constitution there was provision for an elected Legislative Council that would seat fourteen Fijian members, twelve Indian members, ten 'General' members (European, Chinese, and mixed races not included under the other two categories) and four Official members. At the time of writing there can be no certainty regarding the extent or nature of the changes that may be made in the new constitution to be worked out during 1970 to provide the basis for independence, but the communal divisions recognised by the 1966 constitution in this way are of fundamental importance in Fiji affairs. They show every sign of remaining a key feature of Fiji for many years to come, and therefore the basis of this division, and the political results of its expression in this way, require close study.

Political Power
In terms of political power, ignoring the four non-elected official seats, the position of the three groups under the 1966 constitution is as shown in Table 9.

Table 9   *Legislative Council Seats, by Racial Group of Members under 1966 Constitution*

Racial Grouping	Population 1968	Seats in Council
Europeans, part-Europeans, Chinese, and part-Chinese	27,000	10
Fijians and other islanders	229,000	14
Indians	256,000	12

The result of this distribution of political power is that a governing majority cannot be secured by the representatives of any one racial group operating alone on communal lines; it can only be secured by an inter-racial party or by two communal groups operating together. This result, which could be achieved

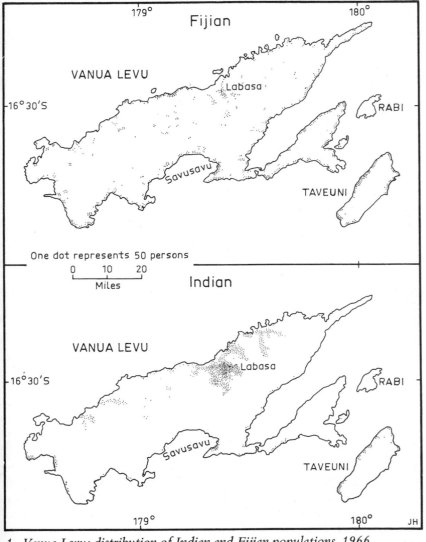

1. Vanua Levu: distribution of Indian and Fijian populations, 1966

even with a considerably smaller representation of the Europeans, part-Europeans, and Chinese group, mitigates against the danger of the blatant preference of the interests of one racial group at the expense of all others, but in doing this the political influence of the European, part-European, and Chinese community is raised far above its numerical significance to a position more in accord with its economic significance in the nation. This has caused some discontent in certain parts of the community, particularly, but by no means exclusively, amongst the largely Indian membership of the Federation Party.

Whatever the criticism that may be made against this, or any other, constitutional device to deal with the racial problem in Fijian society, there is no doubt that the underlying problem, to which these political devices are an attempted answer, reaches deeply into the social and economic life of Fiji. The three groups so recognised are distinct not only in race and political representation. They also have distinct historical backgrounds, different cultures, different motivation and social values. The geographical distribution of the three population components have different patterns; they own different quantities and types of land, which they use to a considerable extent in different ways; their economic roles follow quite different and readily identifiable patterns; they have different degrees of access to different types of economic opportunity. Space will not permit a discussion of all these differences in this small book, but a brief look at some examples is necessary to the subsequent argument.

Geographical Distribution

First, there is the geographical distribution of the population. The European, part-European, and Chinese group is very largely an urban population. At the 1966 census 86 per cent of the Europeans, 84 per cent of the Chinese and part-Chinese, and 71 per cent of the part-Europeans were living in urban areas. On the other hand, only 39 per cent of the Indians and only 24 per cent of the Fijians were urban. The Indian population outside the urban areas is concentrated heavily in the sugar-producing areas of Western Viti Levu, and in the old sugar-producing area of the Rewa River valley, and in the sugar-growing areas of north Vanua Levu. This is clearly shown in Fig. 1. The Fijian population, on the other hand, is very much more widely and evenly spread over the rural areas, a large part of it in regions as yet served poorly, or not

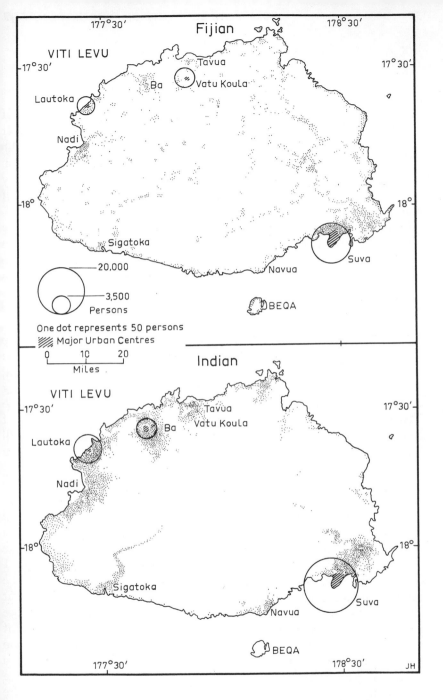

2. Viti Levu: distribution of Indian and Fijian populations, 1966

at all, by the main road system. The pattern of Fijian distribution is illustrated for Viti Levu in Fig. 2. In the other main island, Vanua Levu, the widely dispersed Fijian pattern is equally pronounced. In the lesser islands of the group the proportion of non-Fijian population is generally very small indeed.

Land

Second, there is the distribution of land ownership and use. Only about one-tenth of the land in Fiji is privately-owned freehold, and all except a very small proportion of this is land originally alienated to foreigners before the Deed·of Cession of 1874. Some 83 per cent of all land, amounting to approximately 3,750,000 acres, is owned on a communal basis by over 6,000 Fijian land-owning units. The balance is held by the government as Crown land. However, the alienated land now under freehold is the land originally selected and negotiated for by the settler-immigrants, mostly European, before Fiji became a British Crown Colony, and thus includes most of the land best suited to the cultivation of the cash crops the settlers then considered most likely to be profitable. From the point of view of present-day commercial agriculture, the judgment of those original settlers still looks good, and the land they selected still includes most of the best commercial farming land in Fiji.

The Indians, on the other hand, own very little land, although they farm something approaching 450,000 acres of the best land in the country, including most of the land producing sugar. Of the Indian farmers, more than 80 per cent are tenant farmers, leasing land from Fijian communities, from the Crown, or from other freeholders such as the Colonial Sugar Refining Company. Leases of suitable land are hard to get, competition is strong, and as families increase the pressure from young men and women from Indian farm families having to find careers outside farming, increases in urgency every year. Indian farming is, therefore, of necessity commercially oriented, with the strongest incentives to succeed in commercial farming, for the alternative to success is often the loss of the farmer's lease and a return to abject poverty for the farmer and his family.

With most of the best commercial farming land alienated or

leased out, the Fijians are left with some moderately sized pockets of good land in areas designated as native reserves, and in areas often remote from good communications. They have still quite substantial areas of less fertile or rather steep land suitable for their traditional, shifting, or long-fallow type of subsistence agriculture; but the majority of the Fijian land is unsuited to permanent cultivation and is regarded mainly as potential range-type grasslands and timber areas. In most Fijian-occupied regions there is still sufficient land to sustain a high level of subsistence living at the cost of only two or three days labour a week, but with increasing population, and particularly with increasing small-scale cash cropping to provide supplementary income, the subsistence gardens are being pushed further into the poorer and steeper soils, and it is clear that in many areas the labour input necessary to sustain the accustomed level of subsistence production by traditional means will increase over the next decade.

However, it still remains true that most Fijian villages have sufficient land to maintain their traditional, rather easy-going, level of living, and to accept back into the village community without undue strain people who have failed at, or have merely tired of, wage labour or other commitment to the advanced, exchange type of economic activity outside the village.

Economic Roles
Third, there is the racial pattern of economic activity, which reflects the results of many of the other factors. Here there are further differences between the racial groups. Table 10 shows one major aspect of this pattern. In 1966, 45 per cent of the economically active Fijian population were engaged wholly or mainly in subsistence agriculture, and were thus only marginally in contact with the advanced monetary sector of the economy. A further 20 per cent were engaged wholly or mainly in commercial agriculture or in other primary industry (such as mining). In neither of the other two racial groups was there any significant part of the economically active population outside the monetary sector, and whilst 51.3 per cent of the Indians were engaged in

primary industry, virtually the whole were engaged in commercial farming.

Table 10 *Economically Active Population by Racial Group and Main Industrial Categories*

Industrial Category	Fijians No.	%	Indians No.	%	Europeans, part-Europeans, Chinese, and part-Chinese No.	%
Total economically active	56,154	100	58,705	100	7,426	100
Subsistence agriculture	25,405	45.2	105	0.2	112	1.5
Other primary industry	11,480	20.4	30,035	51.2	1,049	14.1
Total primary industry	36,885	65.7	30,140	51.3	1,161	15.6
Secondary industry	1,976	3.5	5,529	9.4	1,201	16.2
Construction	2,473	4.4	4,317	7.4	365	4.9
Commerce	1,301	2.3	5,446	9.3	1,667	22.4
Transport, hotels, entertainment, etc.	2,288	4.1	3,814	6.5	953	12.8
Administration and government	1,632	2.9	1,071	1.8	340	4.6
Education and nursing and ecclesiastical	3,086	5.5	2,341	4.0	698	9.4
Other professional and allied occupations	626	1.1	645	1.1	425	5.7

Source: Derived from 'Report on the Census of the Population', *Council Paper No. 9 of 1968* (Government Press, Suva, Fiji), T186, 167-199.

Even more striking, if one combines the four most buoyant groups of industries into which most of the foreign and domestic new private investment is being directed—Secondary Industry, Construction, Commerce and the group serving the tourist industry (Transport, Hotels, Entertainment etc.)—we find that over 56 per cent of the economically active Europeans and Chinese group were engaged in these industries in 1966, and over 32 per cent of the Indians, but less than 15 per cent of the Fijians.

Looked at in another way, of the 31,326 people engaged in these outstanding 'growth' industries, 61.0 per cent are Indians, 25.6 per cent Fijians, and 13.4 per cent others (Europeans, part-Europeans, Chinese, and part-Chinese—hereafter referred to as European/Chinese). But this does not properly indicate the

relative participation because it does not distinguish between a
manager and a messenger boy, nor between a small Fijian village
store and a large business with many branches all over Fiji. Table
11 attempts to take into account differentials in status within
these growth industries, and to show better the importance of the
European/Chinese group in the higher paid and supervisory type
of role, and how a very much larger proportion of the Fijian
participation in these industries is confined to the least skilled and
lowest paid categories of employment.

Table 11 *Distribution of Economically Active Population in Most Rapidly
Growing Secondary and Tertiary Industries—by Race and by Status within
Industry*

	Fijians No.	%	Indians No.	%	Europeans part-Europeans, Chinese, and part-Chinese No.	%
Proprietorial, managerial, executive, supervisory and clerical	941	11.7	4,595	24.1	2,449	58.5
Skilled workers	2,016	25.1	5,424	28.4	667	15.9
Semi-skilled and other workers	5,081	63.2	9,082	47.5	1,073	25.6
Total	8,038		19,101		4,189	

Source: Derived from 'Report on the Census of the Population', *Council Paper No. 9 of
1968* (Government Press, Suva, Fiji), T19.
These figures represent the summation of the totals in these categories for Industries
classified as Secondary Industries, Construction, Commerce, Transport and
Communications, Other Service—Excluding Personal, and Entertainment. Figures for
'Personal Service' have been excluded.

What Table 11 does not take into account is that many of the
Fijians included are managing or supervising in small village stores,
and that many of the Indian stores are small to medium size and
many of the Indians owning or managing a transport business
comprising one taxi or one truck are included in the top grade,
whilst many European- and foreign-owned businesses are large
corporations of international standing. When this is realised it

becomes clear that the European group's participation in these growth industries is considerably more important than even Table 11 suggests, whilst that of the Fijians is even less. In fact, it has been estimated that in 1969 roughly three-quarters of the turnover of all Fiji firms, and three-quarters of their new investment, in all industries, is accounted for by overseas companies!

The picture that emerges is roughly that of a 3-tier society in which the European/Chinese group manages and operates the large corporations and institutions, often on behalf of foreign owners, the Indians own and operate most of the medium to small-scale enterprises, including most of the commercial farming, whilst the Fijians own most of the land and are still very heavily engaged in a non-monetary, but affluent, subsistence sector. All are well off by comparison with many similar groups in other lands of the less-developed world.

Access to Opportunities

In terms of money incomes and access to the means of increasing incomes, the three groups differ widely. The Europeans and Chinese clearly have the highest cash incomes *per caput,* and through their existing high level of participation in the most prosperous and advanced types of enterprise, their special skills and experience in large and complex organisations, and their racial and cultural affinity with most of the foreigners who control overseas investment, are in the best position to benefit from the current boom in secondary, tertiary, and particularly tourist industries.

The Indian group is less wealthy *per caput,* though some individuals are very wealthy indeed. Half the economically active Indians are engaged in farming, but new land is exceedingly difficult to get under present conditions, so with the rapid increase in population the majority of the increase in farm families must seek employment outside the home farm, in secondary or tertiary industries. The Indians live either in and around urban areas or in fairly closely settled farming areas usually well served with community services, schools, and communications and with good access to many of the areas in which rapid development of the advanced sector of the economy is taking place. They frequently have friends or relations successfully engaged in business or in skilled trades, from whom they can get guidance and assistance. What is more, they come from families whose activities and economic environment are almost wholly oriented towards the monetised economy, and the young Indian setting out in trading or wage earning has no new and unfamiliar sets of values affecting food and accommodation and other necessities of life to cope with.

For the Fijian the situation is different. In terms of physical and psychic wellbeing he is probably on average still rather better off than the average Indian, at any rate if leisure and security are reckoned of value, though in terms of money income he is much poorer. His traditional way of life, as we have seen, provides him with food, shelter, amusement, security, and has many unique features that he values and in which he takes pride. He believes, and many non-Fijians would agree, that the world will be a poorer place if the Fijian way of life is completely abandoned and lost. Fijians wish for success in the monetary economy and for the rewards and luxuries that money alone can bring within reach, but there are many barriers. Their geographical dispersal means that for a large part of the Fijian population the booming industries are farther away, more difficult of access, and the opportunities more difficult to hear of and get to in time to compete effectively with people from the other groups. Many are faced with psychological barriers, in that the advanced sector of the economy appears to them to be a sphere in which success is won not by the exercise of the generous virtues of Fijian traditional (or indeed Christian) morality, but rather by its opposite. There are many other difficulties, such as generally less familiarity with money as a means of livelihood, less ready access to good schools and good teachers due to their remote situations,[1] lack of communications and amenities, and lower money incomes from which to make the contribution to 'Committee' schools that earn government

---

1. In a valley in Mbaravi I met a Fijian farmer with three children of school age living five miles up a track from the main road and six miles from a school. A school bus ran up the track daily, but the fares for three children five days a week came to more than the farmer's average earnings from cash crops, and though he was otherwise reasonably well off, with a sufficiency of quite good land and a good house, the children did not attend school.

support. There are fewer Fijians successfully established in business and in the higher paid positions in the advancing industries, from whom the newcomer can obtain help, guidance, and perhaps influence in the early stages.

Motivation
There are significant differences also in the patterns of motivation by which the three racial groups are driven.

The European/Chinese group have brought with them and retained the culture and economic attitudes of the commercially sophisticated societies from which they have come. The model of economic man, for whom maximisation of cash income and maximisation of welfare are widely assumed to go together for policy purposes in western economic planning, and which seems to work sufficiently well over a useful range of economic activities in western societies, probably works equally well for this group in Fiji. The result is that the average member of this group is strongly motivated to succeed in economic activities that produce a high income.

The Indian group is similarly motivated, except that a large proportion of them are very much closer to the poverty line, and for these the urgency of their need to earn a money income is more desperate. For the Indian, whether on a farm or in other trade or industry, the alternative to success in the money economy is only too often hunger and dire poverty. Every Indian family must succeed in establishing at least one or two of its members in good money-earning employment, and many families save and scrape for years in order that one or two more promising members may be provided with the capital or the education required for a particular trade or profession. On the land the Indian farmer would normally have no difficulty in adding to his labour input, through family or hired labour, but access to more land is often very difficult and expensive, and sometimes quite impossible. As a result, land tends to be the scarce and limiting factor in his production, and he is strongly motivated to maximise his returns to land at the cost of labour and capital.

For the Fijian, the motivation, both for the individual and for the family, is on average less strongly oriented towards success in the money economy than it is with the other racial groups. A money income is keenly desired by most Fijians, and in recent years the keenness of this desire has undoubtedly been increasing. However, it is desired in the main for the acquisition of goods and services which, if it comes to the pinch, can always be done without. At one end of the spectrum, money is desired for improving their housing, for better schooling for their children, or for investment in a vehicle or a store. At the other end, it is required for cigarettes, tinned foods, and visiting the bright lights of Suva. Unlike most Indians, the average Fijian who fails in commercial enterprise or in wage earning is not faced with abject poverty and hunger for himself and his family. He is merely faced with the need to abandon the bright lights and to move back to the subsistence sector, where a reasonably comfortable, secure, and adequately provided living, with many fewer hours of work, remains accessible to almost all.

For the Fijian who leaves his village to seek employment in the trade or industry of the advanced sector, motivation other than the maximisation of total income is often a major factor. For young men, it may be a desire for adventure, to see the bright lights, to escape from the restrictions and obligations of his junior village status. Many, young and old, may need money, often a specific sum, for a village project, such as building a church, or for the fulfilment of a personal ambition such as the acquisition of a bullock or a farm implement. Whatever the motive, the newly emergent young Fijian is normally only qualified for lowly paid types of wage employment to start with, for he lacks experience and the special skills of the advanced sector. On this low wage, his overall standard of consumption can only be maintained at a level comparable with that of his village, if he receives regular gifts of food from home or if he lodges with relatives. As a family man, the position is far worse, for in wage employment the family usually cannot help, and by working long hours six days a week the unskilled wage-earner cannot hope for years to earn enough to afford a standard of food and housing for all his family that would compare with what they can all have in the village for two or three days work a week. The result is that, within a year or two at the most, many young Fijians return to the village before they gain the experience and skills necessary to raise their earning power significantly. This is not because the Fijian is lazy or inherently less able but because he is rational. The subsistence affluence which led to the import of the first Indian labour into Fiji nearly a hundred years ago still operates to deter Fijians from long-term commitment as wage labour in the advanced sector of their economy.

Now this affluence of the subsistence sector, operating in this manner, has disadvantages. For the individual, in the short term and even in the medium term, it is rational to bounce back to the sector where he is better off. But in the long term, and for the Fijian race as a whole, it has very serious limitation: economic growth as we understand it is only possible in a monetised exchange economy. The growth of specialisation, the division of labour, the accumulation and effective employment of large quantities of capital, and all the major means of enhancing productivity and incomes can only develop extensively with exchange and the use of money. For all practical purposes the subsistence sector, however affluent, is essentially stagnant. The economic advancement of the Fijians therefore is confined to that relatively smaller part of their activities that reaches out into the exchange sector. It is for this reason that, whilst the other racial groups in Fiji are taking part in the vigorous growth of the advanced sector of the economy, the Fijians are being left behind, and the more rapid the rate of growth achieved, the more rapidly will the Fijians fall behind.

A Potentially Dangerous Situation
Racial relations in Fiji have been surprisingly good, but when the factors outlined in this chapter are all put together it is clear that there are dangerous sources of inter-racial tension developing in the situation.

The numerically very small European/Chinese group has enormous economic power in the country, controlling all the larger organisations and enterprises and most of the dealings with the outside world. They also have great political influence which, even if their representation under the new constitution is greatly reduced, seems likely to be sufficient to make it difficult for any likely grouping of parties to govern without their support in the near future. This influence has been, and still is, used in support of the rapid development of Fiji's advanced sector and of making Fiji an attractive place for foreign enterprise and capital.

The Indians have a majority in numbers, but not in political representation. They need the rapid expansion of secondary and tertiary industries to provide employment for the very large numbers of new workers coming on to the labour market, but as this will not be enough to go round, they also need access to more or to improved land. Without this, and even with it, considerable unemployment is inevitable, with falling standards of living and hunger and poverty for many. The Indians have a conflict of interest with the Fijians, not only because they need more land but also because, even without particularly strong competition from Fijians in the advanced sector, there would not be sufficient opportunities to go round. They have a conflict of interest with the European/Chinese group because it has largely been European attitudes, and European/Chinese political influence, that have maintained the Fijian minority in political control and, amongst other things, helped the Fijians to resist further Indian claims for land reform. The European/Chinese economic dominance of large enterprise, and of dealings with the outside world, is also resented, the more so when, as with forest enterprise, the demands of efficiency through economies of scale lead to the replacement of small Indian enterprise with large foreign, and thus normally European controlled, corporations.

For the Fijians, the dominant factors are that they now see themselves to be a minority in their own land, with a booming economy in which they play only a minor part, with political power dependent on agreement and support of one of the other racial groups, with pressure of population and competing uses for land bringing the end of subsistence affluence in sight, and the power of the British Queen, on which they have counted much in the past, now being removed. They have a conflict of interest with the European/Chinese group and with the Indians over the speed of development of the advanced sector, which is running too fast for them to catch up. They have a conflict of interest with the

Indians over land and over the fear of Indian numbers leading to Indian political control, which has led them into an alliance with the European/Chinese group—with whose economic interests they have the least in common.

This is a situation of great potential danger. Despite the good relations of the past, the strains have increased in recent years, and the inevitable growth of unemployment and underemployment during the next decade can hardly do anything but make them worse. This is particularly disturbing at the time of independence, when the one reasonably disinterested arbitrator in the affairs of Fiji is being removed. It is vitally important that this danger be seen and averted, not only because overt racial strife is in itself such a frightful and damaging matter but also because the two main engines of economic growth for Fiji, the tourist industry and the growth of foreign investment, are virtually dependent on the absence of serious racial disturbances. Economic policy to develop such industries at the expense of racial harmony would not only be self-defeating: it could destroy the basis even of the present level of economic activity, and set the economy back two or three decades.

5 Planning and Progress–the Present Path

IN THIS CHAPTER some of the components of present development planning and policy will be examined in more detail, and their effect on the problem of racial imbalance assessed. First, however, it is necessary to reiterate the limitations of agricultural expansion under present policies, and the increasing dependence of the nation as a whole on employment outside agriculture to absorb the very large cohorts of young men and women who will come on to the market during the next decade. This involves looking at the numbers of young people expected to leave school over the period, and the possibilities open for their absorption.

The 1966 Development Plan included a projection of school leavers for 1969 and for 1975. The figures were 12,190 for the year 1969, and 15,910 for 1975, an average over the six years of about 14,000 a year. If one were to assume an approximately constant rate of increase in school leavers over the decade to 1980, then the 1975 figure could be taken roughly as a mean for the period, so that the number of school leavers over the decade may be something approaching 160,000.

Table 12 *Employment (Incomplete figures)*

Year	A No. reported in manual employment	B No. of established civil servants	Total A and B
1960	23,869	n.a.	n.a.
1961	21,589	4,623	26,212
1962	22,835	4,877	27,712
1963	23,854	5,238	29,092
1964	25,805	5,540	31,345
1965	28,745	5,791	34,536
1966	28,522	6,213	34,735
1967	30,698	6,821	37,519
1968	32,959	7,197	40,156

Source: Derived from Bureau of Statistics, *Current Economic Statistics,* January 1970 (Suva, Fiji), T4, 4.

In this connection, Table 12, which gives the available data on wage employment, is of interest. The figures are incomplete, in that they do not include some types of wage and salary employment and they exclude all self-employed. For the census year 1966, Table 12 accounts for 34,735 persons in employment out of a total economically active population of 125,809. However, after excluding those engaged in primary industry (the great majority of whom are self-employed or in jobs not reported as wage employment), we are left with 56,405, of which 5,235 were recorded in the census as unemployed, leaving 51,170 economically active in those sections of the economy offering the main opportunities for wage employment. This calculation gives some perspective to the employment figures as a guide to total wage employment in the economy.

These figures make apparent why it is no one really believes that the Fiji economy can expand rapidly enough to absorb in wage and other money-earning employment the cohorts of young men and women who will be leaving school during the coming decade. Over the seven-year period 1961 to 1968 the increase in employment reported in Table 12 was 13,944. In 1966 the total economically active population, including subsistence agriculturalists and unemployed, was 125,809. In the coming decade the numbers leaving school will approach 160,000! It is this problem that prompted the Governor in his address to the Legislative Council on 14 April 1969 to say 'Urban industrial employment cannot provide employment on this scale, and we must therefore look to the rural areas to make an increasing contribution to the economy.'

Whilst this is certainly true, the question remains as to how that contribution is to be made. There is danger that the rural Fijian village population will make a disproportionately large part of this contribution by absorbing increasing underemployment and so suffering a lower standard of living. To what extent, if at all, this is avoidable will be considered in the subsequent chapters.

In the abovementioned address, the Governor summarised present development policy in these words: 'Priority in development planning is being given to the promotion of growth in agriculture [i.e. commercial agriculture], industry and tourism'.

Let us now re-examine some of the details of this policy for its likely effects on the problem of racial imbalance.

With regard to agriculture, let it first be emphasised that there is no provision in the current five-year plan for channelling any new resources or technical aid into the improvement or extension of subsistence agriculture. On the contrary, over the years it has been the policy of government, through its Department of Agriculture, to treat subsistence agriculture as a brake on development and as something to be ignored and put up with until it can be done away with. This policy is understandable enough under the circumstances, but only partially correct in its premises. It is one that urgently requires some re-thinking, and some constructive suggestions in this direction will be made in Chapter 7.

The prospects for the development of commercial agriculture have been touched on in Chapter 3, where the opportunities for increasing agricultural exports were shown to be not particularly promising. They amount to a modest secular expansion in the market for sugar, of which Fiji hopes to secure its share, but this could probably be adequately provided for by increasing productivity and efficiency on existing sugar farms. There may be prospects for grain sorghum, probably mainly as a second crop on sugar farms, as the external economies of the Millers' organisation and services may be necessary to enable this competitive market to be served. Coconut products have also some prospects for export expansion, though here again the prospects appear to lie mainly in the rehabilitation and improvement of existing coconut plantings, and the battle against the rhinoceros beatle will have to be fought on an ever-widening front. Oil palm is a doubtful prospect, as over-supply of the world market for this product appears almost certain. Coffee and cocoa have similar problems. There is nothing very exciting in the export prospects that seems likely to modify the economic imbalance between the races.

The main prospects for agricultural development, therefore, lie in import replacement and in the expansion of the local markets. The scope here lies mainly in rice and dairy products. In this connection two very large development projects, for which international finance will almost certainly be available, are under preparation. These are an irrigation and drainage proposal for the

Rewa River valley and a development proposal for the Navua River valley. At the time of writing, the financial implications of these two proposals are not yet known, but an early estimate made in 1969 suggested a figure of something over $4 million as a basis for assessing the rough order of financial commitment in which government might be involved.

These two projects alone would, it appears, enable Fiji to become self-sufficient in rice, and possibly also to a large extent, in conjunction with further industrial development (for the production of dried milk and ghee), in dairy products. However, most of the land to be developed in these two projects is either already owned by non-Fijians or is leased and cultivated by non-Fijians. It is unfortunate, but a fact, that these, the only two major agricultural land improvement projects in the whole of Fiji that at present seem practicable and economically sound are, by accident of history and geography, so located that Fijian farmers are not in a position to benefit much from them. If implemented, therefore, these two projects, which in all other respects appear so promising, will benefit mainly the two non-Fijian groups in the population, and will directly act to worsen, rather than improve, the economic imbalance between the races.

Timber is another rural industry with substantial prospects for growth and development. It falls into two distinct types of development. First, there is the exploitation of the indigenous forests. Here production comprises the extraction and processing of a resource already there. For reasons explained in Chapter 3 the exploitation of these timbers will be confined in the main to a few large-scale, well-capitalised, and efficient operators, and will become increasingly capital intensive. This almost certainly means a substantial proportion of overseas capital and control. The income from this industry will go largely to capital and management. There will be some labour component, but this will be relatively small and unlikely greatly to affect the relative economic balance between the racial groups.

Mining, similarly, is becoming more capital intensive, though the Emperor Gold Mining Company has for a considerable time been the largest individual industrial employer of Fijians. There are at present about 1,000 Fijians so employed, due mainly to the success of a deliberate policy of the company to recruit and retain Fijian labour. This they have done, where so many other large employers have failed over the last century, by providing the conditions in which the Fijian can become a member of a permanent and committed labour force, gain in experience, skill, and productivity, and throughout feel himself better off materially than in his subsistence village environment. This has been achieved not by paying cash wages widely different from the market rate but by providing accommodation and services of a good standard at moderate cost, including such items as electric light, garbage disposal, water supply, and for a time rations purchased in bulk and supplied on credit through the company store. Most important of all, the company provided separate married accommodation for workers with families, together with a small area of land for cultivation as a subsistence garden. These provisions enabled the committed worker to keep his family in much the same way as he would in the village environment, producing most of their own food; the standard of services was usually better than in the village, and most of the worker's wages could be used to raise his level of living above the village subsistence level. There have also been other factors in this success, including effective and enlightened paternalistic attitudes of management, but the former were the main ones, and without them the others would have had little effect.

Expansion of mining by the Emperor Company, if it occurs, would presumably follow this same pattern, but this is dependent on the price of gold and on suitable new ore bodies being found. Other possible mining expansion, including off-shore oil drilling, is as yet largely an unknown quantity, except that a large proportion of the income will necessarily accrue to capital and to imported skills, and it appears unlikely to be a very important source of local incomes through direct employment. It seems reasonable to forecast, however, that unless the special type of measures taken by the Emperor Company to encourage a committed Fijian labour force are adopted, the difficulties already described are likely to limit the participation of Fijian rural labour.

In secondary and tertiary industry, including especially those components associated with tourism, rapid expansion will provide employment in the advanced sector of the economy for considerable numbers. To this will be added the construction and transport work associated with new investment in these industries. In all this part of the economy productivity and incomes will rise. However, with the job vacancies inevitably falling so far below the numbers of people of all races seeking remunerative employment, the competition will become even keener than it is now. Under these circumstances, wherever the normal processes of private selection are unimpeded, those with the best qualifications, best and most relevant experience, best access, best contacts, and those able to hear of and apply for the opportunities first, will have the advantage. Where opportunities arise for establishing a service or a business, those with access to capital will also have the advantage, though those with capital but lacking the other qualities will soon lose their capital in competitive operations on the open market. In all these respects, and in the strength of their motivation to compete and succeed in these particular fields of endeavour, the advantage lies on the average with the non-Fijian racial groups. The result is that, with freedom to compete, non-Fijian dominance in these industries, and especially in the more remunerative roles, will continue and will increase.

In some important respects policies in the public sector reinforce this tendency. Understandably, though seen with the wisdom of hindsight perhaps inadvisably, public policy has been to grant maximum assistance in social and educational facilities to those areas and institutions that offer to do most for themselves. The education system of Fiji is greatly influenced by this policy, as the government provides and operates only about forty schools in the whole of Fiji, out of a total of 701. By far the majority of schools in Fiji are 'Committee' schools, for which funds have to be raised by a local school committee to the extent of half the building and equipment cost and 10 per cent of the salaries of trained teachers. Until a few years ago the proportion of the teachers' salaries contributed by the local committee was required to be 25 per cent.

This policy has had some good effects. It has certainly made the government budget on education spread much further, though the total cost to the community has not, of course, been thereby reduced. The main effect, however, has been to ration the scarce resources available for education in such a way that those prepared to make a larger contribution secured a larger share, including a larger share of the public contribution. Although some special treatment has been given to help village areas, especially in the remission of fees, it nevertheless remains a fact that those communities prepared to pay the quickest and the most got more classrooms and more teachers. This perhaps is fair enough, but it does tend to mean that the remote villages with poor communications and little regular income from the cash economy, however willing, have been less able to contribute than areas of prosperous cane farms and dormitory areas for the wage and salary earners of the towns. As a result, these areas where the need and difficulty of entry to the advanced sector is greatest tend to have the least effective educational facilities for that purpose, whilst those already effectively commercialised have the best. To some extent the same type of problem arises in other fields of social development, where the wish of government to encourage and reward local self-help tends to favour the already more prosperous areas in many respects. As a result, the Fijians tend in general to have poorer communications, and less access to electricity, piped water, health services and other amenities than the other components in the population.

The largest individual development project yet proposed, the new, sealed Nadi to Suva road, to cost some $12 million, operates in this way also. The benefit will go to the tourists and the tourist industry, to car and vehicle owners, to transport companies, business and service industries, in all of which the Fijians in the main play only a small or a lowly part. The rural Fijian living along the line of the road will benefit to some extent from improved access to Suva and Lautoka, and from lower freight rates for his produce, but the numbers so affected are relatively small, and the benefits from the sealed road as compared to the present less comfortable and slower but still serviceable road are quite small.

The present path to development is thus one which, looking at the Fiji economy as a single unit, secures a high level of growth in product and in employment opportunities with the resources and markets available. In this respect, planning has been and is being effective. From this point of view the decision to concentrate on commercial agriculture, on secondary and tertiary industry, and in particular on the tourist industry, is sound. So also is the proposed expenditure of $12 million on the Nadi-Suva road, and the possible $4 million on the Rewa and Navua River valley developments. So is the forestry program, and the concentration of technical agricultural resources on cash cropping to the exclusion of subsistence agriculture. All this is wise and sound if you look at Fiji as a single unit.

As we have seen, however, Fiji is not in fact such a unit. There is serious racial imbalance in the economy, and serious strains exist between racial groups because of the conflict of interests between them. The present planned path of development, with its emphasis on 'the promotion of growth in commercial agriculture, industry and tourism', *through the very effectiveness of the plan and its implementation,* is rapidly worsening this imbalance and adding to the strains, at the very time in Fiji's history when it is least able to stand it. This is bringing into jeopardy not only the economic growth the plan seeks to produce but also a large part of the social, political, and economic progress won over the last few decades.

6 The Proper Objectives of Economic Policy

ECONOMIC POLICY is a course of action pursued by a government in the sphere of economic activity, and the immediate objectives of such policy may be economic ones. However, the ultimate objectives of economic policy, and the results of economic action, are concerned with the whole structure and activity of society. They cannot be treated as a separate and distinct compartment in the life of the nation.

It is a strange feature of the world today that vast resources are devoted in every sphere to the problem of how to do things, but very little to the problem of what to do. The latter is often taken either as being so obvious as not to require serious attention or as being outside the proper orbit of scientific and rational investigation. The result is that man is equipping himself with almost unimaginable power to modify his environment in the achievement of ends that are selected almost without thought.

The formation of economic policy in Fiji is no exception. Over the last decade much attention has been paid to providing the political and administrative machinery for the preparation and implementation of economic plans. There is a Ministerial Development Planning Committee under the chairmanship of the Chief Minister, a Central Planning Office with a staff of economists and other experts in the Ministry of Finance, and smaller expert groups in other ministries. To these have from time to time been added the specialist resources of international consultants and of teams from British and United Nations institutions. In this way the capacity of the Fiji government to assemble, co-ordinate, and direct the resources of the nation in pursuit of economic development has greatly increased, and indeed a high level of efficiency in this direction has been achieved.

But the purpose or end to which this powerful and efficient machinery has been directed has been accepted more as a matter of faith than of deliberate and careful choice. It is as though government has accepted for the nation a counterpart to the model of 'economic man' which economists use, sometimes with serious imprecision and lack of definition, as a simplifying assumption in economic analysis. In other words, government appears to have taken for granted that a 'rational' nation is one that will maximise its national income, and that this indeed is the path to the greatest good for the nation and for the majority of its component people.

It is doubtful if this unqualified assumption is sound in any circumstances, but in Fiji it clearly is not. It might, perhaps, be reasonable to say that, other things being equal, maximum economic growth is beneficial—but other things never are equal in a world where economic change affects also the structure of social and political life. If a government wishes to institute a policy of development and change, it is necessary to realise that the political, social, and economic features of the life of the nation are merely different aspects of the same human relationships. It is just not possible to meddle with one without producing some modification in the others.

Difficulty arises when means are confused with ends. If the aim of government policy is to make Fiji a pleasant place for its people to live in, then an increase in the national income may be a useful component in the set of means by which that end may be achieved. If, on the other hand, the aim of government is to increase the national income, it is perfectly possible that this end may be achieved most quickly and efficiently by means which also make Fiji an intolerable place in which to live.

The proper objectives of economic policy are those that will contribute most towards the attainment of the type of society and environment desired. For this reason, a long clear look is required at the precise specifications of the society and environment to be produced. Without this, the situation is analogous to that of a ship in which all resources are devoted to the improvement of the engines and to driving them at maximum speed, on a course set by guesswork. This policy can be disastrous for any ship in Fijian seas, and a slower and more devious course would normally produce better results. So, in the formation of the national policies of which economic policy is to be a part, speed of economic growth must not be allowed to usurp the position of an end to be maximised for its own sake; it must be treated only as one of the potential means to achieving the desired ends, and adjusted not for maximum speed but for maximum achievement in the desired direction. In Fiji, as in the reef-obstructed seas around it, full speed ahead is the almost certain course to disaster, and a slower and more devious course is certainly to be preferred.

The precise definition of the society and environment desired is not something that can be done quickly or easily. It certainly cannot be attempted here. It is something that requires at least as much expert care and attention as the preparation of the economic plans to which it should give direction. All that can be done here is to draw attention to the need, and to urge that the necessary resources be directed without delay to its fulfilment.

However, in illustration of the theme, it is possible to mention some key parameters that must certainly be contained in any such overall specification, and to consider some of their implications for economic policy. One is the management of Fiji's own affairs independent of Great Britain. This could not long be avoided even if one party or the other were reluctant. Another is the maintenance of racial harmony, the failure of which would bring suffering and poverty to all communities. A third would be population control, without which Fiji's limited land resources must become overcrowded. A fourth might be to abolish the worst poverty, which is not necessarily the same thing as to create new wealth. These will do for illustration.

Given the achievement of success in these directions, an increase in the average income *per caput* may be a desirable objective also, but advancement in the direction of these parameters is more important than the increase of income, and growth measures that tend to prevent such progress must be postponed. In fact the main economic problem requiring massive and urgent government intervention in Fiji is *not* the size of the national income but its distribution, and this requires recognition at all levels.

However, this is an oversimplification and it is necessary to specify the economic aims in more detail. It is clear that racial tensions amongst Fijians stem not from the immediate danger of abject poverty and hunger, against which they will be cushioned over the next decade by their land rights, but from their loss of economic, and to a lesser extent political, influence in their country, and from their inability to take a reasonable share in the growing advanced sector of the economy. Their growing resentment against the two other racial groups needs to be relieved by a rapid improvement not merely in their total but even more in their proportionate share in the economic activity of the advanced sector.

Amongst the Indians, the chief danger to racial harmony stems from the fact that even the rapidly expanding secondary and tertiary industries can absorb only a part of the increments to the Indian workforce that will accrue during the decade, and that the stark alternative of grinding poverty and hunger will face rapidly increasing numbers, particularly if measures to increase Fijian participation in the advanced sector are successful. These tensions need to be eased by providing a less stark alternative; and greater access to land, even for raising subsistence crops, is one important means of doing this.

The European/Chinese minority have nothing to fear except resentment of their economic pre-eminence, resentment of their disproportionate political influence, and the damage to the economy that would result from any kind of racial strife. However, this is a very real danger if tensions continue to mount indefinitely: not only their future profits, but their property and their very lives could be at risk. This is the more so because, in their role as a small but highly favoured minority, whose economic position is a source of envy in both the large racial groups, they would almost certainly be the first target against which the irrational forces of violence would be directed when tensions reach breaking point. Their situation is such that a slowing down of their present rapid gains in prosperity, if it helps to reduce racial tensions, should be carefully weighed against the alternative prospect of very much heavier losses a little later.

Under these circumstances, the proper objectives of economic policy certainly include, at very high priority, measures to draw a greater proportion of the Fijian village population into the advanced sector and to assist them to gain the experience, skills, and other requirements to qualify for higher places of responsibility and income there. Similarly, it must include greater access to land for Indians unable to make a livelihood in secondary and tertiary industry. Above all, it must include the fullest support for measures of population control to prevent the indefinite prolongation and magnification of these problems. These objectives are more urgent and vital than increments to the average income *per caput* of the nation as a whole. The attainment of these objectives should have absolute priority in calls upon the efforts and resources of the nation, and not just receive what remains after implementation of measures for 'the promotion of growth in commercial agriculture, industry and tourism'.

What is more, these criteria for the employment of the resources of the nation should apply equally to the natural resources, including timber and minerals, and to use of foreign capital and enterprise. In all these matters, whether the enterprise concerned is off-shore oil exploration or resort development for tourists, the effect, now or later, on the prospects for solving those major problems, rather than just the effect on the total national income, must determine national policy towards them. This does not mean rejecting or discouraging foreign enterprise and capital, but it may in some cases modify the terms and conditions upon which it may be sought. For example, for the exploitation of mineral resources an enterprise operated along the lines of the Emperor Gold Mines, which makes a deliberate and substantial contribution towards the amelioration of the problem of Fijian participation, is far more valuable than one that does not, and it could be sound economic policy to insist on such an approach in the exploitation of any such resources, even if this delayed or initially reduced the efficiency of exploitation. Similarly, in the exploitation of natural timber resources, the value of the efficiencies and economies of very large scale might (though this is less certain) be outweighed by the disadvantages of capital intensity and foreign control.

In the application of these criteria, and in the pursuit of what has here been called the proper objectives of economic policy, there is involved a change of emphasis in the direction of economic planning and development. This will involve, from all racial groups, some considerable sacrifice of interests that now are jealously guarded. From the European/Chinese group may be demanded some reduction in their relative economic and political power, and possibly the postponement of some opportunities for profitable expansion. It may also be necessary for them to accept, in some directions, increased costs and lower efficiency in some enterprises they own or control, while they introduce and train more Fijians at all levels. From the Indians may be demanded the patience to accept the expansion of Fijian labour and enterprise into opportunities for which they themselves are available and better prepared, and to see a larger share of government resources devoted to development of the more remote rural communities in which Indians have little part. From the Fijians may be demanded further access for Indians to some of the unused lands upon which, for the last century, Fijians have believed their security to depend. Nor are these by any means the only sacrifices that will be involved. However, this is a necessary path, to which the alternative is exceedingly grim for all concerned. In the words of Professor Watters,

'Little hope remains for Fiji unless all racial groups and especially the Fijians act now, with vision, resolution and self-sacrifice to subordinate their narrow, sectarian interests to the interests of the country as a whole.'[1]

---

1. R. F. Watters, *Koro* (Clarendon Press, Oxford, 1969), pp. 279-80. My italics.

IT IS ALL VERY WELL to talk about the proper objectives of economic policy and the application of new criteria in the process of policy formation, but if the objectives and the criteria are not practicable in real life, they are of little value. The purpose of this chapter is to show how, by redeploying the resources actually available or accessible to the Fiji government, it is possible to direct economic development constructively towards the amelioration of the most urgent and critical problems of independent Fiji, and so fulfil the proper aims of development policy. It is also hoped to show that it is not too late to start; that if the problems are frankly faced, and the necessary 'vision, resolution and self-sacrifice' applied, the resources available are sufficient to attain those objectives.

In doing this, no attempt will be made at completeness. That can only be attempted in the planning unit, with its greater resources of staff and information. Here it will suffice to illustrate, rather than to specify in detail, how such aims can be fulfilled. Moreover, only the three most pressing objectives will be discussed—population control, Fijian participation in the advanced sector, and Indian access to land.[1]

Population control is necessary because Fiji is without question a labour surplus economy, and is likely to continue so in the foreseeable future. It is a simple mathematical fact, therefore, that the lower the growth of population can be kept, the wealthier the people will be. Population growth rates of 3 per cent per annum merely mean that people in the future will be 3 per cent poorer *for every year that this rate of growth continues* than they would have been had the population remained static on a self-replacement basis. Where population control is practicable, there

1. The successful solution of the problem set by the withdrawal of the Colonial Sugar Refining Company ownership of the South Pacific Sugar Mills, discussed in Chapter 3, will be assumed.

is no economic development measure that offers so assured an improvement in income per head.

Fiji has already instituted a public program to this end, and results appear encouraging. No further discussion is proposed here, except to point out that, so long as there seem reasonable prospects for increasing the effective spread and impact of this campaign, it should never be allowed to lack for the necessary funds.

The other two objectives are in certain respects closely inter-related. The first is to get the Fijians to take a larger part in the economic activity of the advanced sector at all levels. This means in commercial agriculture as well as in secondary and tertiary industry, and involves getting Fijians into work that would otherwise be undertaken mainly by Indians. It is therefore related to the second objective, which is to improve land utilisation, particularly in the subsistence sector, in order that land may be available both for the expansion of commercial agriculture and for lease to Indians, without causing an effective scarcity amongst the Fijians. This will involve the intensification of agriculture, a process that is necessary also for the achievement of important parts of the program in support of Fijian participation. The measures required for the achievement of these objectives will be considered in two parts, rural development, and non-rural development.

Rural Development

In planning rural development it is necessary to recognise that for most Fijians at present this is practically all development. Therefore, if the Fijians are to take a larger and more effective part in non-rural industries and activities, then the planning for that participation must start in the rural areas.

The non-rural Fijian population is still relatively small and much of it is transient, for it includes a considerable number for whom the excursion away from the village will not last for more than a year or two. The very small number of Fijians who are permanent and committed in non-rural employment does not provide an adequate base on which to build the hopes of the Fijian people for adequate participation in the more advanced economic life of their country. The innate abilities required for special success in that sphere are a variable factor among individual members of any population, and although they must be supplemented by training and opportunity, the numbers likely to achieve such success will be very much greater if that training and opportunity are accessible to the whole Fijian population and not just to a small elite.

The required program of rural development therefore needs to achieve a number of subsidiary aims. These include the obvious ones of making village farming more productive and making the rural areas a better place to live in. But it must also provide for a large offtake of Fijians from the villages into secondary and tertiary industry, and must make it possible for these people to be better prepared and better qualified for such participation when they get there. It must give them better access to the urban and other areas outside the villages where the opportunities for that participation are greatest, and it must enable them to be in closer communication with that non-village world and to know quickly what is going on there. It must bring new ideas and incentives to the village farmer, and better training and preparation for his work, so that increased productivity and prosperity·will reach him as well as the *galala* and the other workers who leave the village.

A two-pronged approach is therefore necessary, designed on the one hand to raise village participation in commercial agriculture and associated enterprises, and on the other to enhance Fijian participation in non-rural industries. A policy of simply syphoning off the cream of Fijian enterprise and productive manpower from the rural areas, leaving only the unskilled and the idle, would be wrong. Increased efficiency and welfare in the rural base are necessary parts of the total program, without which other major objectives cannot be achieved. Therefore it is fundamental to both parts of this program that the facilities and amenities available to the village populations be increased, not merely to make them better places in which to live but also to make them better places from which to start out into careers in the more sophisticated sectors of the economy.

The first component of rural development must therefore be to provide better communications with the outside world — roads, buses, postal services—together with better schools, better teachers, and better housing and facilities for teachers. These make up an expensive program, and such amenities cannot be uniformly supplied at public expense in all areas at once; but the priorities must be clear. They are more urgent and more important in remote areas where the people have little money income than they are in areas that can afford substantial contributions in capital building funds and in fees or rates. They require a reversal of some existing bases of allocation, and will divert resources from other more favoured areas in accordance · with the objectives of economic policy. It is a wrong system of priorities that prepares to spend $12 million or more on improvements to the Nadi-Suva road, and only a few hundred thousand on new access roads to Fijian village areas. The major resources of the Fiji government and of the Fiji economy should be devoted to the most pressing needs with absolute priority.

The next component in rural development is to increase the level of rural productivity. This needs to be considered in two parts:

(i) the intensification of subsistence agriculture; and
(ii) the development and extension of commercial agriculture.

Both are important, and both require intervention with substantial resources by government.

Subsistence Agriculture. In many respects, Fijian subsistence agriculture, in common with subsistence agriculture in many areas of the Pacific, is well adapted to its environment, highly productive, and efficient in the use of those resources that, in the normal village context, have been scarce. It is perhaps largely for this reason ·that there has been so little government intervention directed at its improvement. However, this has been in the context of abundant land. The Indians in Fiji, being acutely short of land, maximise returns to land and use it, in this sense, more efficiently. The Fijians, being rich in land, have not needed to do this; for them, to maximise their returns to labour rather than to land has been the rational aim, which they have achieved remarkably well in many areas.

However, with increasing populations and increasing alternative uses of land (for cash crops), unaccompanied by any likely substantial increase in the total quantity of land, a change in this situation appears inevitable in virtually all Pacific territories. This is so in Fiji, particularly as the postponement of heavy pressure on Fijian subsistence lands has been due to artificial factors, including the Fijians' own relatively slow adoption of cash cropping, but above all to effective exclusion of the heavy Indian pressure for land from the great part of Fijian subsistence land. Within two decades, the abundance of land for subsistence production, which is the basis of the efficiency of the present techniques of subsistence agriculture, will have disappeared. Therefore, a change from extensive, long-fallow techniques to intensive continuous cropping seems inevitable in all the Pacific region, and should be prepared for. In Fiji it is necessary that this process of intensification be brought forward in time, in order that land may become available for the many other purposes for which it is so urgently required. This demands that considerable resources of agricultural research capacity, extension services, and institutional supports (providing external economies and common facility services) be concentrated on the intensification of village subsistence agriculture and its conversion from extensive long fallow to intensive continuous cropping techniques.

The first major requirement is research. This is an area of development in which very little has yet been attempted anywhere in the Pacific. As a starting point, excellent opportunities for initiating this research lie in artificial environments outside the existing village pattern, where some form of intensive subsistence agriculture has been attempted already for many years. The subsistence gardens allotted by the Emperor Gold Mine Company to its married Fijian staff at Vatu Koula, which have been cropped continuously, though at much reduced levels of production, for over twenty years, seem to present one such an opportunity.[2]

2. Apart from the appropriate agricultural features of this area, offering some hundreds of individually operated lots, in large contiguous groups, and on land not remarkably fertile, the organisational factors favouring research are outstanding. Communication with the Fijians concerned is particularly easy; the organisation of joint activities, bulk supply of inputs, provision for credit and collection of payments, the provision of transport, machinery, and even aircraft services are readily arranged; and the active co-operation of the mine administration would greatly facilitate and extend the effectiveness of a small research team.

Whatever the locations, the main problems requiring study are quite clear. There are agronomic problems associated with the preservation and replacement of the fertility of the soil, the prevention or correction of erosion, and the maintenance of the texture of the soil with subsistence crops under conditions of continuous cropping. Then there is the question of control of disease, whether bacterial, viral, or fungoid, and the control of insect and other pests, all of which require new degrees and techniques of control. Other research requirements include selection of new varieties better adopted to the environment of the continuously cropped garden (e.g. disease resistance, fertiliser response) and the possibilities and economics of the use of legumes or other rotation crops that may produce not only a contribution to the food of the family but also to the nutrients in the soil. Finally, in the application of all these practices, a study is required of the managerial and organisational requirements for making the new inputs available and applying them efficiently and on a practicable and profitable basis. To this end, the maximum use of economies of scale, through co-ordination and co-operation, the use of common facilities, bulk buying, and the necessary institutional arrangements to make them work, requires thorough investigation and some experiment; for not only do such practices render considerable economies available in the cost structure but they can also greatly increase the effectiveness and returns from the measures taken.

The resources needed for the initial stages of this problem will not be quantitatively very large, though in some respects the qualitative requirements may be difficult to fulfil. It is, however, a problem potentially of very wide application throughout the Pacific region, and one for which the assistance of international organisations would be readily available. Ultimately resources of a different order may be required to implement the results of the research, as for example through the establishment of some institutional basis such as Farmers Associations on the Taiwan model or through public or semi-public institutions for the administration and finance of land intensification schemes, but the nature and extent of such requirements cannot be assessed at this stage. The intensification of subsistence agriculture is, however, an essential development not only for the expansion of commercial agriculture amongst the Fijians but also, as will be seen, for the easing of key Indian problems and for getting increased Fijian participation in the non-rural industries.

Commercial Agriculture. In the development of cash crops much has already been done, and the technical services of the Department of Agriculture are excellent. Here there remain many problems in the Fijian village areas, of which those of distance, communications, and other basic facilities have already been discussed. There are problems of finding suitable crops for expansion, problems of land tenure and control, and above all problems of motivation and of organisation. But basic to all is the need for intensification of subsistence agriculture. Each excursion into cash cropping tends to displace the subsistence gardens from the better land to the less fertile and steeper slopes, where the length of fallow needs to be longer, and the labour input greater, for the maintenance of the required level of food production. The result is that the opportunity cost of cash cropping on Fijian village lands is continually rising. The removal of this growing disincentive, through intensification of subsistence cropping, is a vital step, urgently required.

Beyond that, the chief problem is to bring to the Fijian farmer the economies of organisation and scale necessary to make small-scale farming viable. This was originally done for the cane farmer in that magnificent symbiosis between the foreign owned and controlled milling company and the Indian and Fijian smallholders who grow the cane. Without the wide range of services provided by the milling company, the Fiji sugar industry could never have been established as a smallholder industry.

For some major agricultural industries, either with high capital costs for processing, such as tea or palm oil, or with special marketing and grading requirements, such as tobacco, the establishment of a smallholder basis for production is virtually impossible without some institution to provide these types of services and co-ordination on a large scale. Sugar is by no means alone in this regard. However, even in less exacting crops, such an institutional background, which ties marketing, technical services, credit, and supply of inputs together in one co-ordinated operation, is most advantageous to the farmer, particularly where his resources and his experience are both limited. The best means for such provision must be explored in all rural development planning, and what is technically and organisationally possible must be provided. This is another case where very high priority must be given to claims on available resources.

The nature of these claims, however, may vary greatly with the precise circumstances of the individual set of needs for an industry or a region. The South Pacific Sugar Mills pattern is almost unique. In Fiji, some of the tobacco companies have to some extent attempted an approach along these lines, but generally speaking with less favourable results for the farmer and with a smaller range and scale in the services provided. These patterns have the advantage, from the point of view of government planning, that the resources required for the establishment of these institutional services are provided from private sources, and often largely from foreign private sources. The nuclear estate pattern has somewhat similar advantages, and has been used with some success in other countries with oil palm cultivation and with tea. However, complete reliance on foreign private enterprise in this respect also has disadvantages, in that some degree of monopoly or oligopoly is almost inevitable, and uncertainty about the political or economic future of the industry can lead to a sharp conflict of interest between the large private firm and the smallholder, which can become difficult to control.

Other possible methods of providing these services include large-scale directly managed land-development projects of the type so successfully operated by the Federal Land Development Authority in Malaysia; these are excellent for the purpose if the resources of capital and skilled technical and managerial man-power are adequate. It is questionable whether this is yet practicable on a large scale in Fiji, though the possibility of obtaining financial and technical assistance from international organisations for this purpose should be explored. The applicability of the Farmers Association approach, with adequate legislative preparation in the grant of legal powers, should also be examined, though at first sight it seems doubtful whether Fijian village society would readily adapt to such a system.

On a smaller scale, there is a role for co-operative societies, though their missionary role fits them more for a gradual long-term adaptation to the methods of the advanced sector rather than the rapid mass transition required by the Fijian situation at independence. Nevertheless, so long as the necessary entrepreneurial and managerial talent can be provided from outside to complement the modest internal resources of the societies, institutions such as the Valley Industries Co-operative in the Sigatoka valley will fulfil a useful role. So also will the direct intervention of government-operated institutions, such as the Banana Marketing Organisation and the organisations operated by the Department of Agriculture for the marketing of vegetables and for assisting in the development of cattle grazing projects.

All these methods require consideration. The ultimate selection in any case will depend on the individual needs and circumstances, and on the resources available. The important matter is to recognise and accept the principle that small-scale farmers in the Fijian situation cannot institute a large-scale movement into commercial agriculture in a short period of time without very substantial institutional assistance of this kind. They need organisation, direction, co-ordination, and their resources need to be supplemented with the skills, capital, plant, and management required to weld them into an industrial unit with economies of scale; and the unit must be able to operate an efficient system of transport, distribution, and marketing, and to manage and secure their credit needs, and to deal on their behalf, as a unit, with government departments, markets, the Development Bank, and other institutions. Without this, there is no possibility whatever of effecting the necessary transformation of Fijian village agriculture in the time available. With it, as some individual successes in a number of Pacific and African countries have shown, it is perfectly possible.[3]

---

3. Further details are given in R. T. Shand (ed.), *Agricultural Development in Asia,* Chapter VIII, published in Australia by Australian National University Press, in America by University of California Press, and in Britain, Europe and the Far East by Allen & Unwin.

Land. Now we come back to the question of land and its availability. It has been clear that the problem is a particularly difficult one,

(a) for physical reasons concerned with the relatively fixed supply of land and its geographical characteristics on the one hand, and

(b) for institutional reasons related to Fijian ownership and custom on the other.

In the section on the intensification of subsistence agriculture, one path has been charted which will reduce the area of land required by Fijians for their village food production. In the next section, on commercial agriculture, it has been shown how some of this additional surplus will be utilised for cash cropping by the Fijians. Of the remainder, some must be made available for lease to Indians to relieve what would otherwise become an intolerable pressure of unemployment and hardship.

This is easy to say, but its implementation is fraught with many difficulties. The land so available will mostly be of poor fertility, and much of it will be hilly. Even if the institutional difficulties of granting usufruct to non-Fijians can be overcome, physical difficulties will remain. The more intensive use of this land will require guidance and assistance from government, both through research, extension, and advisory services specially instituted for this purpose and through the provision of mechanical and other aids for erosion control and the like. It will, moreover, be necessary to accept the fact that in many such areas it will not be practicable to aim at farm sizes that will yield an income comparable with the average cane farm. It will still be necessary, and worth doing, if it can achieve no more than a bare alternative to, or cushion against, unemployment.

Other methods of improving the land situation must also be explored. The Rewa and Navua River valley schemes will make some contribution by increasing the productivity of existing land, provided that a means can be found for increasing the number of farms and the population supported thereon. As a long-term consideration, the possibilities of reclamation of the 100,000 acres of mangrove must also be kept under continuous review.

The institutional problems of ownership and control are particularly difficult, and particularly important. No procedural suggestions will be attempted here regarding the method of dealing with these problems. What has been suggested is an attack on the underlying economic and political causes of the difficulties. Fijian ownership and control extend over very large areas that Fijians have not been able to put to effective use, and they have been increasingly reluctant, as a race, to surrender rights in this respect because it has seemed to be their one remaining assurance of primacy and security in their own country. The other development measures here suggested, by improving Fijian participation in the advanced sector and by substantially reducing the area of land needed for Fijian subsistence, will operate directly to reduce Fijian fears in this respect. These measures thus operate on the psychological and political as well as the physical barriers impeding the provision of a cushion on the land for at least some of the Indians threatened with unemployment and serious hardship. The opportunity so created must be grasped with determination and good will. It must be seen clearly as an indispensable component in the program for the accelerated advancement of Fijians into the advanced sector of the economy, and the procedural difficulties must be overcome. The achievement of independence from the colonial power provides a particularly favourable opportunity for tackling these problems.

Resources and Concentration. The resources required for such a program of rural development are substantially greater than those now allocated to that use, and within the sector itself priorities will differ from those previously applied. The first of the three subsidiary aims, provision of roads, communications, schools, and amenities to remote Fijian village areas, does not necessitate an increase to the total resources now available to government. Whilst such an increase would always be welcome, the essential need is simply for recognition of priorities and the application of available resources to meet the most important and pressing need. The resources should be transferred to this use from other projects of lower priority in other areas.

Resources for the second subsidiary aim, the intensification of subsistence agriculture, are available in part within the Department of Agriculture, to which substantial additions of funds and technical specialists would be available from international organisations for the research and experimental phase. The fact that this is a regional problem of wide significance is of assistance here.

Resources for the institutional support necessary, both in capital and in managerial talent, will be required later. The capital requirement will be modest and in most areas Fijian communal or co-operative methods, with some small assistance from the Development Bank, will suffice. Managerial talent, however, will be the key to success, and will need to be augmented in much the way that the Co-operative Department has operated in the past, but on a larger scale.

For the stimulation of Fijian commercial agriculture, apart from the considerable and excellent technical work already being undertaken by the Department of Agriculture, and the auxiliary measures already described (roads, land, etc.), the main new requirement is for the institutional backing. This will require quite substantial resources of capital, managerial talent, and skills. The manner of its supply will depend on the type of institutions deemed most suitable in each case, but in the main the choice lies between foreign private capital or loan funds from international organisations, with either being supplemented to a lesser extent by local resources. Initially it will be necessary to obtain managerial and technical talent also from outside Fiji, to supplement and train what is becoming available locally. Both capital and personnel will be fairly readily available, from either type of source, provided racial harmony and internal good order can be maintained.

Finally it is necessary to emphasise the importance of concentration of effort in all these measures. The cumulative effect of a number of discrete but complementary measures in different fields at the same time greatly enhances the speed and extent of the results achieved, and is an economy in the long run. Everything is in favour of the 'big push' approach to these urgent problems, and everything is against the current use of inadequate palliative measures that do not reach to the heart of the problem. The suggestion that the Fijian village economy, with a little exhortation and organisational assistance, will be enabled 'from its growing resources, to strengthen and enrich its own social provision, in education and housing and health and recreation—in a word, to develop itself,'[4] is no more than wishful thinking where the rate of development necessary is exogenously determined by the extremely rapid development of the modern and urban sectors of the economy. What is required in the field of rural development is not just a stepping-up of present procedures but rather a complete change of emphasis in the allocation of the total resources available for development.

Non-Rural Development

Under the heading of non-rural development, two main sets of problems will be considered. The first is that of Fijian participation in secondary and tertiary industry, together with that part of primary industry that tends to be capital intensive and to be conducted outside the village areas, such as mining. The second is the problem of policy towards non-rural development that does not contribute directly to the solution of the prime problem of Fijian participation.

Attention will be confined in the main to the problem of Fijian participation. This is not because it is the only problem by any means, but it is the one problem outside the village areas that requires an entirely new level and type of approach. As has been made clear in Chapter 5 and elsewhere, systematic planning for the advanced sector of the economy outside the villages has in other respects been very efficient, and therefore requires little detailed comment here.

Fijian Participation. The problem of Fijian participation can be considered in three sections. First, there is the question of how to get Fijians into such employment in substantially greater numbers than at present; this is the problem of access. Second, there is the question of how to retain them in the advanced sector as a permanent workforce so that they continue to grow in experience, skill and productivity; this is the problem of commitment. Third, there is the question of equipping them, both before and after

---

4. Guy Hunter, *Rural Development (Organisation and Administration),* Legislative Council of Fiji, Council Paper No. 6 of 1969 (Government Press, Suva), p.8.

they gain access, for other than the lowest paid and least responsible jobs; this is the problem of status.

To none of these problems is there an easy or a universal answer. But this does not mean that nothing can be done. On the contrary, by applying the principle of concentration, and holding in focus a clear image of what is to be achieved and why it is necessary, a very great deal can be done. The process is one of a large number of separate but related measures which, taken together, will have a cumulative effect in the direction of the desired objective. Every available opportunity must be sought out and exploited; every accessible obstacle must be removed or reduced; above all, the process must have the priority warranted for one of the most pressing and vital components in national policy, and must command the full support and resources of government necessary for its effective implementation.

The first step in such a program must be a firm statement by government that a substantial and rapid increase in Fijian participation in the advanced sector of the economy, at all levels, is a major objective of policy. The reasons must, of course, be made clear, and the point made that it is an essential ingredient in a set of inter-related policies, which include the Rewa and Navua projects and the other processes already discussed for increasing access to land for Indians.

Then there needs to be an institution created, with resources, a clear mandate, and some authority, to co-ordinate and implement the vigorous prosecution of this policy in that wide area of activity in which government, individuals, and corporate bodies are all substantially involved. In what follows, it will be called the Institute for Fijian Participation, or the IFP for short, though a more imaginative and inspiring name would be required in practice. Its function would be to undertake and co-ordinate those parts of the program of increasing Fijian participation in non-rural industry that fall outside the normal functions of government departments. The form and detailed operations of this institution will be discussed briefly, after some of the many activities in which it may take part have been mentioned.

From the point of view of the individual Fijian, the problem of access necessarily starts at the village. The need for improving the village amenities and facilities for preparing him for excursions into non-village occupations has already been discussed under rural development. In addition, there is a need for improvement in the flow of information to the villagers regarding the prospects of and requirements for, extra-village employment, particularly in those villages in the outer islands and in other remote areas where travel is expensive and difficult. This is a requirement that the proposed IFP, through its information section, should fulfil. The objective of this service will be to get the right sort of Fijian, with appropriate qualifications, to the place where work for which he is suited, and in which he is interested, is likely to become available.

Beyond this, it is necessary to look at the problems facing the individual Fijian at the other end, that is in the urban areas or in the region of the industry in which he is seeking employment. He has a number of needs that must be fulfilled when he reaches the area concerned. These include information about job opportunities from day to day, contacts and introductions, advice about where to go and how to conduct himself, and food and accommodation while searching and waiting. In this he is no different from job seekers of other racial groups, except that for the Fijian the job opportunities are more frequently remote from his home base, he is less familiar with the principles of living in the advanced sector, and the urban facilities available through family connections and friends tend to be more restricted. The number of well-placed Fijian families able to provide such hospitality and services is small. Most villages have very few such contacts available, and these may not be in the right place or may not have the right experience or contacts to meet the needs of many would-be job seekers. In addition, there are sometimes, for this very reason, excessive calls on the hospitality of the few that are well placed, causing severe strain to the families concerned, and this itself can retard the further advancement of promising Fijians who have had some initial success. In all these respects, the Fijian is less favourably placed than members of other racial groups, and this is therefore a point that requires intervention.

The mobility of Fijians into secondary and tertiary industry will thus be greatly facilitated by the provision of some kind of hostel accommodation at strategically located points in and around the main towns, with good and cheap transport connecting to the main centres of the industries concerned. These hostels should provide only for workers without families. In addition to food and shelter, they should provide information, guidance, and help in the search for employment and in retaining it. Guidance and help in managing their affairs in the new environment, and in handling money and credit, should also be offered. Charges must be kept as low as possible, and could perhaps be waived for a limited initial period whilst employment is being sought. Initial capital would best be provided through the IFP, which would administer and operate the hostels and provide the ancillary services.

However, whilst this will help with the problem of access, more elaborate provisions are necessary to keep the Fijians in such employment—to deal with the problem of commitment. To this end, provision has to be made for a man to be able to live with his family, and to do so in circumstances that compare favourably with the standards available in the village.

In this, the approach used so successfully by the Emperor Gold Mining Company provides a major part of the answer. In addition to hostel accommodation for single workers, the company provides married accommodation, with services, and above all small *teitei* or subsistence garden allotments, for married workers and their families. Where new industries are established requiring substantial labour forces away from closely settled areas, this type of provision would not be difficult to arrange. The need for a resident labour force in such an area makes the provision of some kind of accommodation essential in any case. Experience at the Emperor mine has shown that, even with existing agricultural techniques, the required effect can be achieved with the allocation of quite small lots of a quarter of an acre and less for a family, and with the implementation of the measures already discussed for assisting the intensification of subsistence agriculture the effectiveness of such small lots will increase.

In the urban areas the provision of this type of facility is normally the function of a housing corporation, for which there are models all over the world. To meet the special needs of this program, however, a unit with special characteristics is required, and it would be better provided by a branch of the proposed IFP.

The requirement is for very low cost housing on a rental basis, with access to a garden allotment of about one-eighth of an acre per house unit. The garden areas should have certain common services provided to facilitate intensive cultivation, including fertiliser application, pest and disease control measures, and such regulation as may be necessary to ensure good husbandry. Where it is necessary to locate such settlements outside the immediate town area, special provision will be necessary for bus and other transport services at a cost and frequency suited to the needs of the settlement. This should normally present no difficulty for arrangement with normal commercial operators, but where subsidisation of transport costs seems necessary in the initial stages, this should be provided.

Finally, it is necessary to consider what can be done to deal with the problem of status. This again falls into two parts, the first concerning the improvement of the Fijians' qualifications before they start work, and the second concerning the improvement of their qualifications and opportunities for promotion after they have started to earn their living.

The first starts with secondary schooling and trade training, and for a few goes on to the provisions for tertiary education. Education beyond primary standard is always a difficult problem for rural areas, in Fiji as in most other countries. It just is not possible to have secondary schools and trade schools within a mile or two of every village.

Decentralisation of such schools to rural market towns is satisfactory only to a very limited degree. Too great a dispersal of scarce teaching resources reduces standards, and too great a distance to travel daily to school, even if provided free, tires and strains the child and reduces his performance. No second-best or improvised arrangements are adequate to meet this need. Therefore the provision of boarding scholarships on a very generous scale for Fijian village areas is necessary, as is equivalent boarding accommodation. This need applies to trade schools and apprenticeships as much as to secondary schools. For at least a part of this requirement the proposed IFP should be made responsible, for it will be more economical and more effective to provide central IFP-operated boarding arrangements, from which

Fijian students could attend the various schools as day boys and girls, rather than to provide special additional subsidies to numbers of schools, some of which may not normally have boarding facilities. Such an approach would also have the advantage of removing this special provision from the normal run of scholarships allocated by open competition. The purpose of this particular provision is quite different from that of normal scholarships, in that it is designed specifically to enable those whose environment has left them at a disadvantage to catch up with those who have had better opportunities. Hence the basis of allocation cannot be by open competition amongst all races, or even amongst all Fijians, for not only is it likely that the remote rural villages will have fewer facilities to enable a student of innate ability to compete effectively with his town competitors but it is a waste to allocate such resources to children whose circumstances do not make them necessary.

The second part of the problem requires close liaison with employers but needs attention to be extended also to self-employed Fijians operating businesses and trades on their own account. There are many posts and types of occupation, particularly those with some organisational and financial responsibility, for which there is a quite widely held prejudice against the employment of Fijians. Sometimes in the past there has been some justification for this prejudice. On the other hand, there are sufficient qualitative exceptions to show that such problems can be overcome. What is required is careful and expert research to identify clearly the nature of the underlying causes and to deal with them by training and by adjustment of environmental problems.[5] To this end it is considered that the IFP should have a training division, with a small but highly competent research

---

5. I saw an excellent example of such an approach in the South Pacific Sugar Mill's 'Cane Development Scheme' at Cuvu, west of Sigatoka, in south-west Viti Levu. This was a special operation conducted under the supervision of a Field Superintendent, Mr Syd Snowsill, which studied in detail the problems of low productivity amongst cane farmers, mainly Fijian, and sought to correct them. Problems of Fijian social organisation and of communal land tenure, as well as problems of an economic or educational nature, were all met and dealt with. This operation had had quite spectacular success, and over a period of a few years in many cases had succeeded in getting many almost completely unproductive Fijian cane farms to levels of production comparable with those of established Indian farms.

section whose function is to identify difficulties impeding Fijians from advancement in individual trades, businesses, and industries, and to provide in-service or part-time training and assistance to overcome the problems. Training provision should include short specialist courses for improving efficiency, operating for two or three weeks at a time, by special arrangement with employers, and covering a wide range of occupations. Examples might be courses to improve the efficiency of retail store attendants, courses in bar management and restaurant supervision, courses in the commercial operation of a truck or taxi, courses for tourist guides, and refresher courses for small businessmen operating their own businesses. A type of facility, found of great value in Malaysia, is a team of bookkeepers who provide a service to small businesses, putting in a simple set of records, showing the operator how to use them, and following up with one or two later visits to resolve problems and advise on difficulties that arise subsequently.

These and many other types of interventive measure are practicable and necessary. Their identification and design will follow easily once the first requirement is met: that of facing up to the real nature of the problem and determining to deal with it with absolute priority. The objective is to get more Fijians into business and industry, and to get them to achieve higher status there. It is quite fatal to the achievement of this objective to pretend that this does not involve giving the Fijians special treatment and help, at least in the short and medium term, for this is precisely the way in which the problem must be solved.

There is useful experience of this type of approach in Malaysia, though what has been done there has suffered severely from lack of adequate concentration and co-ordination and from being applied too late and with insufficient resolve. In particular, the institution of MARA (originally RIDA) and the MARA Institute of Technology provide many examples both of what can and what cannot be done in this way. On the positive side, both have attracted valuable technical assistance from international organisations and private foundations. On the negative side, neither has been permitted to intervene on a sufficiently broad spectrum of activities to influence more than a small part of the factors limiting the Malays' participation in the advanced sector of their economy.

For Fiji, the precise form and title of the institution to provide the necessary direct support for Fijian participation can best be determined by the Fijians themselves, for a great deal depends on the extent to which this organisation can fit in with, and make use of, the existing Fijian institutions from the level of the Council of Chiefs to that of the individual village and its subdivisions. However, some of its essential functions and powers can be specified.

It must have clear and powerful direction. The board, council, or other governing body should be headed by a senior minister, preferably by the Prime Minister himself. In its dealings with government departments or private corporations and industrialists it must be clear that it is operating with the authority of a major instrument of government, and not as a minor subsidiary that can safely be ignored. It must have the means, and the status, to deal at top level with foreign and local companies, and with individual businessmen, in order to engage their co-operation and enthusiasm in what is being attempted.

The institution must be given legal status to hold and administer land, including Fijian land. It must have authority to raise and use loan funds (presumably through the Development Bank in most cases), to enter into contracts, and to operate businesses and services where these seem necessary in the pursuit of its main objective (e.g. to run a bus or ferry service or to operate a store for training purposes). It must have the power to run hostel services, to buy, build, rent, and sell houses, and to operate and control agricultural plots. It must have funds and facilities for providing substantial numbers of scholarships, at all levels up to post-graduate, and to provide boarding accommodation to go with them. It must conduct an employment and information service, maintain close liaison with employers and with Fijian self-employed businessmen, and undertake continuous research into the problems of Fijian advancement in trade and industry. It must provide special training and remedial services to meet the needs revealed by such research.

In providing this institution with the resources necessary to carry out these functions, the co-operation and material support of the Fijian traditional institutions from village level up must, of course, be expected. Moreover, for many purposes, a large part of the funds required should be, in the long run, self supporting—as with the hostel and housing projects. For these, loan funds, even from international sources, may be available, and should be sought, either directly or through the Development Bank. Some support might eventually be found from funds accumulated from Fijian communal activities, including the leasing of some lands. However, it would be a grave mistake to press this self-financing aspect too far. The services are required irrespective of how they be financed, and a large part of the resources required must come directly from the funds available to government for development. These funds must be generously provided, if necessary at the expense of less vital and less urgent development.

Having said that, it may be added that the additional call upon government funds will not be particularly heavy. In many cases, as with the education expenses involved, it will involve rather a transfer of resources from one form of education expenditure to another where it will better serve the main policy objectives. In others, such as employment services, a large part of the machinery is already operating, and all that is required is a small addition to make these services more widely available in more appropriate form to the Fijian special requirements. Given the will, the way will not be particularly difficult.

Other Aspects of Non-Rural Development. For the rest, there is not a great deal that needs to be said. Given priority to the main objectives mentioned, the planning of the advanced sector can then proceed very much as at present. Some reduction or deferment of developments planned will be necessary, to the extent that resources have had to be diverted from them, but this will not be catastrophic.

Provided the measures taken for population control, for intensification of subsistence agriculture, for making land available to Indians, and for increased Fijian participation in the advanced sector of both rural and non-rural industries are successful, other development, including the tourist industry together with all its ancillary services, may be expanded vigorously. Such expansion is only a danger if the other measures are *not* adequately provided for.

Index

Designed by Cathy Akroyd

Maps drawn by Cartographic Office, Department of Human Geography, A.N.U. based on the Legislative Council of Fiji, *Report of the Census of the Population,* 1966

Text set in 12/12 Aldine Roman and printed on Glopaque Wove, 94 g.s.m. by Pacific Computer-Electrographics, Sydney

E. K. Fisk is Professorial Fellow in Economics, Research School of Pacific Studies, Australian National University. He joined the University in 1960 after thirteen years as an administrator and practising economist in Malaya, serving as Chief Economist and first head of the Economic and Planning Division of the Rural and Industrial Development Authority from 1958 to 1960. Since then he has been engaged in research in South-East Asia, New Guinea and the Pacific. He has published widely on planning, rural development, and the transition from subsistence to market economies. In 1968 and 1969 he concentrated much of his attention on Fiji, where his two major specialist interests, a multi-racial society and a large affluent subsistence component, come together in the one economy.

Jacket design by Cathy Akroyd.
Photograph of tapa-cloth
by Visual Aids Section, A.N.U.

Printed in Australia